The Land of the Hazelnuts

Growing up in Tukwila

Fast Eddy

Edited by Karen Sweeney

The Land of the Hazelnuts

First Printing April 2018

ISBN-13: 978-1983622649

FOR

My wonderful parents, my incredible friends, my patient teachers, and for anyone who shared in the unforgettable experiences of growing up in suburban America in the 1960s. In Tukwila, or elsewhere.

And for all those who didn't but would like to find out what they were missing....

CONTENTS

INTRODUCTION

There MIGHT be other places equal to it scattered throughout the universe. But I doubt there was anyplace BETTER for a kid to grow up in.

To today's children, life in the Tukwila of the 60s probably sounds quite alien, even primitive. If a kid had their own phone, it was made from 2 tin cans hardwired with a cotton string. Surely there were no video games on it. The only drones there were, came from our teachers lecturing. And no, we didn't have any GPSs to guide us through life. There was no such thing as a "PC" either. Neither Personal Computers, or Political Correctness.

Long before PlayStation and radio control cars, we created our own play stations all over town. Sometimes at a ball field or park. Other times, we would build our own hydroplanes out of a hunk of scrap wood, to tow behind our bikes with towering imaginary rooster tails. Or we might fabricate a car from old roller skates that we had fished out of a smelly garbage can.

No kid ever has skinned his knee on an X-Box. But getting banged up a little was routine for us. Strangely, we reflect upon the blood we spilled and the tears we shed in our adventures, with nostalgic joy.

Maybe we were like aliens to the modern kids. But we were happy, fun loving aliens. busy prospecting the treasures of this odd, crazy corner of the planet. The placed that the Native Americans before us had called, the Land of the Hazelnuts.

Like the young Indian braves who had climbed the same hills and explored the same woods and fields, we were born free. It was a safer world than now, and we meandered through the brush without fear of predators. Either natural, or human.

It was different to grow up in the big city of Seattle 15 minutes north. Or in the rustic country farmlands of Kent and Auburn a scant 15 minutes south of us. Tukwila was a breath of fresh air barely beyond the soot of Seattle's smokestacks, and a nose length away from the cow pies of the Kent Valley. Suburbia shared the perks of their urban and rural neighbors, with few of the drawbacks of either.

There weren't very many places for our parents to shop in Tukwila. They had to travel to Burien or Renton to find a decent supermarket. Our Dads gladly drove a short commute to get to work. It was by their choice.

People didn't choose a home for its proximity to their likelihoods, or to have their provisions at their fingertips. They chose them for lifestyle. Home was where we lived.

In this suburb, people really lived. It was a place to get away from the hustle bustle of the city, but with the country close at hand too. And for kids, a expanding circle of 30 miles would give us a sample of the mountainous, the aquatic, the urban or the rural lifestyles

Tukwila had the innocence of Leave it to Beaver's Mayfield, combined with the character and charm of Andy Griffith's Mayberry. Yet in the 60s, the traditions of culture were changing quickly to the astonishment of the "Establishment" who had watched progress creep along with the pace of a slug in their lifetimes.

In our generation, the trail of slug slime was drying, and technology was taking off like the jets we built at Boeing. And the dreams of mankind reached beyond our world to look toward landing on the moon for the first time.

For kids like me, there wasn't a care in the world. But the world at large was far from trouble free.

As my friends and I played soldiers in our woods and sandlots, a real war was raging in Vietnam.

Some of the older kids had been drafted before the ink on their high school diplomas had a chance to dry. They were shipped off from the peace of home to terrifying jungles in Vietnam.

Many had barely started to shave their beards when they would be returned to their friends and family in flag draped coffins.

On college campuses there was unrest both over this unpopular war, and in support of people who had been oppressed for centuries rightfully, rallying for equal rights. Walter Cronkite warned of the escalating threat of a nuclear attack that might vaporize our hazelnut trees into mushroom clouds.

As kids, we didn't fully grasp those worries, and any trickle-down concerns about the future would quickly evaporate in the dust of our bikes as we skidded to a stop at the corner store at the bottom of the hill.

We might carry a basket full of empty pop bottles to exchange for a Popsicle on a hot day. But we didn't carry many apprehensions in our minds.

Coasting down the steep half mile slope of 58th Avenue down to the store was a breeze. But climbing back up the hill would require every gram of sugar from our Popsicles to scale it. Those were our challenges and concerns.

But those ups and downs in our little town helped shape us into who we are. If we could have chosen when and where we could land when we were born, I believe most of us would have ended up right where we did.

It gave us all lifelong memories to share, and those memories gave me this book to write. We can't go back, but we can go forward in life with the knowledge we shared in a very special time and place that will never be again.

1

NEW ROADS

Below ground, where no one could see or hear, the bulldozer was trapped like a panicked. wild animal.

Its tracks spun furiously, clawing desperately to get free. Sparks darted through the air as the tracks were grinding on the rocks beneath it, casting faint flickers in the shadows of the dark, dusty cave.

The echoes of the steel biting against rock were deafening, as the jammed rig rattled and rocked in place. A sick, gritty metallic taste swirled in my mouth as I panted with anxiety.

Clumps of dirt were falling from above in small avalanches, landing on my hair and face. Blood trickled down my forehead as a jagged softball sized stone bounced off my skull. .I desperately yanked levers trying to dislodge myself from this rapidly filling grave.

What an ill-conceived, hairbrained scheme I had, to try to tunnel through the unstable silt and clay without first shoring the walls and ceiling.

But there I was, deep in the pit, bathed in darkness, choking on bellows of dust and carbon monoxide. Hopelessly jammed in the narrow dungeon of dirt and stone.

Suddenly, the entire cave shook like a pair of dice in the hands, about to be rolled. It was as though the feet of a giant were stomping on the ground above me. The walls began to crumble in, further paralyzing my bulldozer as I jammed the levers futilely to fight for its freedom.

Beyond fear, I was hysterical in hopelessness. My trembling hand wiped the dirty sweat off my forehead. I wondered if and when this tunnel, might segue into the other tunnel that led to the brilliant light of the next world. Dread consumed me. In the shadows on the dirt walls, I thought I saw images of the grim reaper, sickle in hand, dancing in the strobe of sparks

"No, No...NO! I'm too YOUNG to DIE!." my inner voice screamed to myself. "Please NO, NOOO...! Isn't there ANYONE to help me?" I begged.

But the grim answer came in the sound of a huge gush of water racing my way. The mist from the charging river hit first, chilling the air, and bringing a shiver to the back of my neck.

Just then, the deluge tore into the walls and ceiling of the pit. Sealing the machine, and my fate in a quicksand like flow of cold lava. The bubbling water rising quickly up to the top of the hole.

The last thing that I heard, was laughter.

"QUIT IT Mike! You're getting me all WET" I said dryly, annoyed that he had ruined my play tunnel project, and interrupted my vivid imaginary, pretend construction disaster.

Mike Bergstrom pulled the garden hose out of my dirt hole in his yard and washed the muck off my Tonka Toy Bulldozer. He had been the friendly giant, who had leaped on the ground bringing the earthquake, and Armageddon to my project. And had flooded my dreams, by using his thumb on the full blast water hose.

"Sorry Ed", he smiled. "But, you just seemed to be kind of lost in another world....:"

That I was. But it was a good world. For all of us. Both in our reality, and in our imaginary, pretend worlds. Where no matter how deep our imagined predicaments were, we could always wash off our hopelessness, with a blast of the hose.

We had good inspirations for both building both pretend roads, and reenacting floods. In the winter, the Duwamish River would often over run its banks, near the Longacre's Horse racing track. Burying the Dairy Farm in its currents.

The roads disappeared, submerged by the expanding flow of the river. The only thing that distinguished the vast body of water from a lake, were the heads of cattle bobbing up from their underwater pastures. And farmers in rowboats tossing bales of hay into the drink.

Meanwhile our new freeway, Interstate 5, was just being built. My friends and I were among the first to travel down the yet unopened lanes on our bicycles when the construction workers went home for the day.

And some of our local girls also trotted along those same trails with their horses. Leaving hoof prints, and smelly piles of manure to greet the road workers the next morning.

We saw our friends move away, and whole neighborhoods being mowed down by the graders to make way for the freeway.

At the same time, all of us were changing too. As we were growing up fast, and paving fresh new roads in our young lives

As a boy, it was fascinating to watch the mammoth machinery carving out valleys for the road, reinventing the face of our city. A few things were preserved, as they cleared the land for I-5.

Normally rocks don't roll uphill, but the famous "Foster Rock", somehow made the climb from the freeway excavation, up steep, formidable Bremmer's Hill. To rest eternally on the lawn beside the Foster High School's parking lot

The "Rock" was an iconic boulder that had been a landmark of graffiti for as long as anyone could remember. It was more paint than rock by the time I came around.

It meant enough to someone, to spare it from the freeway demolition machines. Every Fosterite was fond of our colorful boulder. The big stone was cocooned in many layers of paint, and school spirit. It was the very first, "Pet Rock".

There wasn't as much graffiti sprayed on walls, bridges and sidewalks as there is today.

The Rock's graffiti wasn't malicious. It was affectionate. The "bad" graffiti was found printed in pen or magic marker on bathroom walls.

And even most of that wasn't necessarily offensive or mean spirited. Much of it was funny or clever, reading material to enjoy while taking care of business.

The Rock changed color like a chameleon as students would constantly update the paint, paying homage to their class year. Purple with white lettering (or white with purple), the colors of the Foster Bulldogs, were top selling hues at the paint store.

Styles were changing too. The flattop crew cuts of the 1950s were beginning to creep down our foreheads. And the girl's hemlines were beginning to rise from the knees, as Poodle skirts and swing dresses were being replaced by miniskirts.

Our voices were changing. The jargon of the 50s, "beat" generation was heading off into squaresville, as we left the "Dolls" and "Daddy-O"s back at the sock hop. We had new things to say, and a new way to say them.

The landscape was changing, not only with the freeway, but my new shiny new grade school, Tukwila Elementary was also nearing its grand opening.

For those kids who lived in central Tukwila, it would be a welcome transfer from the drab hallways and classrooms of Showalter, aka the "Pink Prison" This new school looked like a minimal security facility at best.

Southcenter, the world's largest shopping mall at the time, was about to arise from the swamps in the lowlands of Tukwila and put us on the map.

I'm sure the "old timers" lamented these changes. Just as I do when I see my own favorite haunts disappear. And see them replaced by unfamiliar structures intruding where they once stood.

But to us kids, those changes were exciting. We loved to see the progress in the progressive world we lived in.

One place where progress was slow to arrive, was on the pavement of the Tukwila streets. Auto repair shops loved our roads. They helped them sell lots of shocks and front-end alignments. But drivers hated them. Tukwila was the "chuckhole" capitol of the world.

The good thing about chuckholes, was there was never any shortage of mud puddles to stomp in on our way home from school. Thanks to the Seattle rain, they were almost always full to the brink.

We learned early how to stomp in them with a sideways foot, to direct the spray at our friend's pants legs. After all, what are friends for?

5

One of my earliest friends was Mike Bergstrom.

Many of my early days were spent at the Bergstroms. Road construction was just a small part of my daily routine. There was a newness in life, and a fresh excitement in almost everything we did. With so much to do, if you were bored, it was no one's fault but your own.

The Bergstroms had four acres of land to the north of our own acreage. Both properties showed evidence of their earlier days as farmlands. They each had leftover chicken houses. The Bergstroms even had a dilapidated barn. You couldn't ask for better buildings to use as camps or playhouses.

Roosters would crow, in the distance, announcing the break of day, Mary Bergstroms horse would scent the air with the essence of a farm too by returning his hay to the ground from which it came. So, you could not only see and hear the country life in the suburbs, you might even step in it, if you weren't careful.

Two thirds of the Bergstroms spread was pasture land. In the summertime, I would be dwarfed by the tall yellow straw that spread from the Moore's north of the Bergstroms, to our own property line. The stalks towered over my head. hiding me as I was trudging through that well-worn path that connected the Bergstrom's house with my own.

But in the early days I was usually at Mike's, or at home, or somewhere in the straw between us.

Mary Bergstrom's horse, Sonny could eat hay around the clock, and never make a dent in their pasture's seemingly limitless supply. My parent's acreage was about one third woods, another third house and yard, and the final third overtaken by the advancing wild blackberries. Blackberries owned the place.

Blackberries were the most savage of plants. Ruthless and determined, the tentacles of blackberries reached far beyond their roots. Aggressively choking out any form of life in their path. Watching closely, you could even see them grow.

But I was grateful for their malignant growth. Because cutting the grass was my livelihood. That's how I earned my allowance. The more blackberries we had, the less lawn there was to mow.

Sometimes Mom would send me out picking. The blackberry pies she baked would be delicious. But it didn't come easy.

I spent hours baking in the hot sun trying to fill a big coffee can with the little berries for the cause. Of course, it would have taken less time if they hadn't tasted so good. The little picker had to eat while he picked.

Between the woods, the pastures, the river, the ponds, farm buildings and the blackberries, there was always some place to be. And something to do, to keep a kid amused right in our own neighborhood.

Like the Indians who came before me in the Land of the Hazelnuts, I knew every trail, tree, bee's nest and fern in my woods. I had our woods charted in my mind like a map maker. I had even named its landmarks.

There was "Split Tree Branch" where a maple tree had been struck by lightning and the fallen branch had made a natural bridge over a ravine. "Rock Valley" where the trees stopped growing, and the sun shined through the thick foliage. And "The Junkyard", where an old car from the 1930s was rusting away under a cover of moss and vines.

Amid the rodents, rabbits and squirrel rustling in the brush, the one thing I never feared, was "bad guys" hiding out in the woods.

Kids felt safe to roam about in Tukwila. Times were so much different.

It was a rare time in life. We were yet unburdened by responsibilities, pressures, or even concerns about our own safety.

We lived adventurously without a net to catch us or a script to guide us. The purpose of life was to have a good time. There would be plenty of time to find plots for our stories later. This was to the time to explore and enjoy.

Beneath the arching, thorny, blackberry vines, my friend Lon and I made an elaborate system of tunnels. It was great fun to explore through the mazes hidden by the brush. Until I came upon a wasp nest deep in that jungle of sharp, prickly stalks...

Then I realized how hard it is to move quickly on your hands and knees through stickers. In my hurry to escape, I would earn a set of scratches on my face and a dozen bee stings to remind me of the location.

Carl and Kay Bergstrom both worked full time, so their six latchkey kids were raised uncaged and free range.

There weren't as many rules there as in my house. I think that was one of the things that made hanging out there so appealing for me. Not that they did anything terrible.

They just had the liberty to experiment and try different things without the surveillance of a Mom or Dad looking over their shoulders all the time.

I'd often start my day with breakfast at the Bergstrom table. Mostly, it was Cheerios, but thanks to Taffy, their black and white Collie, I would mix it up once in a while with a couple handfuls of Purina Dog Chow straight from the bag. It was the Bergstrom kid's idea.

Dog Chow isn't bad. It tastes kind of like a dry, ground up, meaty hardtack. What its meat by products meant or what species they were, who knew? Who cared? Taffy loved it. Might as well see what we were missing out on.

They say you don't look a gift "horse" in the mouth. You just eat it graciously. Thanks, Bergstroms! But eating it a few times made me glad that I was a human being, and not a dog.

My sister tells me that the Bergstroms had an indoor sandbox in a room all its own, But I don't remember that. I do recall their cool, old fashioned upright piano. I didn't play, but Mike sure did.

Mike had taken classical piano lessons from an early age, and his parents insisted that he practice every day. Listening from the outside, it sounded like Mozart himself was tickling the ivories on the Bergstrom's ancient piano.

But stepping into their living room you would discover it was just a tall skinny little kid with bright red hair and freckles making all that sophisticated, grown up music.

But the Bach and Beethoven that he played wasn't my cup of tea. I'd rather be out making roads in their yard. And when it came to music, I liked the Beatles and the Beach Boys far better.

With his considerable musical "chops", I had hoped Mike would someday become the keyboard player in some famous rock band. And of course, in my imagination, I would have been the guitar player in it.

But we never, not even once, made it on the cover of the Rolling Stone. While Mike's talents were admirable, but they didn't translate well into rock 'n' roll. And at the time, I didn't even know how to tune a guitar, much less play it.

In the Bergstrom's workshop they had a ping pong table. That's where I learned early about the agony of defeat. Through endless practice, the Bergstroms had all become table tennis masters. Every volley I would attempt would be returned by an irretrievable slam.

Swinging a ping pong paddle in his hand, Mike was on fire. And he looked as though he was too. With his bright red hair whipping around on top, Mike's face glowed as he dominated the games. He was the "Slam Master".

Although the Bergstroms couldn't be beat at table tennis, it was still fun. Sometimes, Mike would let you think you were finally going to finally win a point, then he would humiliate you with some English or a crazy spin. Ping pong at the Bergstroms was always a lesson in humility.

Not just around my house but on every street, every day, the crack of baseballs on a bat, or croquet mallets on a wooden ball echoed through the trees, accompanied by kids yelling and laughing. The sleepy streets were awakened by bands of kids with their youthful energy each day. If it wasn't raining too hard, the streets of Tukwila were never vacant

We knew everybody on every street, at least by their names. And we had heard their backstories. We knew what the parents did for a living. And what their kids did for fun. Neighborhood intelligence was critical. You needed to know which adults would be likely to snitch on you if you were up to no good.

The lawn of the Bergstroms, the Sweeney's in fact every kid's yards, big and small, was well worn from thousands of foot marks. Both human shoes, and four-legged paw prints.

Running, jumping, romping along with us whenever Seattle's weather would permit, most dogs would dwell outside in unfenced yards. Spreading their good natures, their vigorous barks, and their fleas, far and near. Their kid buddies spent most waking hours playing with them in the fresh air.

It was not only a great time to be a kid, but it was also a howl to be a dog then too. Rover's territory didn't end at his yard. It extended as far the kids would go. The love we had for our furry companions indeed rivaled that which we had for our best school friends.

Our dogs would be waiting to meet us after school and walk us home. While we were tied up in the classroom, our dogs had their own little cliques with their canine pals. Running together to chase Rabbit, Moose or Squirrel. (We didn't REALLY have any Moose)

Dogs lived their lives much like their pet kids did. Unlike the highly supervised regimented lives that many dogs lead today, kenneled in a stuffy condo. They have little choice. If they roamed the streets as our dogs did, they would be risking arrest out in the Animal Control's heavily policed streets.

Back then, unless the dog was a real troublemaker, he would probably just wag his tail from the sidewalk as the dogcatcher drove by, waving at him.

Leashes were uncommon, and a dog barking wasn't a capital offense. There was some elbow room between most of our houses. And the conversations of dogs barking at each other was as natural as a chirping robin, or the winds whipping up from the valley through the Maple and Hazelnut trees.

Inside dogs were an anomaly. Most dogs lived on or under our porches. Or else in a home-built doghouse winter, spring, or summer.

Just like me, my dog (named Shamrock), knew every trail, every twig and every fallen leaf in the woods surrounding my house. These lands were every bit his land, as they were mine.

Our watchdogs weren't the pampered toy poodles riding around in the designer purse of some diva, wearing pink wristwatches and jeweled collars, as you see today. They were mutts.

Good old dogs, who found delight simply in riding in the back of a pickup truck or in stomping through mud puddles along with us. Their biggest joy was just to be with their favorite kid. And truly, that feeling was mutual.

The dogs would love to spend the night out in the yard with us as we spread our sleeping bags out under the stars. Sleeping right beside us, keeping one eye open for the "Boogie Man". Occasionally, they would swing by our faces checking on our well-being with a sniff and offering us a sloppy kiss with their tongues.

They were always "Rin Tin Tin" ready to pounce upon any threat or invader, at any time. I think dogs used to watch a lot of "Lassie" because every family dog shared Lassie's affection and loyalty to their "human packs".

The Ken L Ration commercials used to sing," My Dog's BETTER than YOUR DOG, MY Dog's BETTER than YOURS" Of course, he was. To you... Every kid's dog was the absolute best in the world. When you were in trouble, he would be the only one to give your love and lick all your guilt and the pain right off your face.

Even if there were no other friends around to play ball with, your dog kept his calendar open for you 365 days a year. Our hounds rated us as highly as we regarded them. To them, we were flawless.

Today's "Couch Potato" dogs, might lounge by the door sleeping, as the kids whittle away the hours on the X -Boxes. But our dogs took a bite out of life, grasping its fullness in their incisors. Snarling fearlessly at any intruder who dared to step into their jurisdiction. They were family members in every sense of the word, other than their sleeping accommodations.

Cats were, back then as they always shall be. Stingy with their affection, temperamental, and a little bit conceited. Not picking on the kitties. To me, the lifestyle of Tukwila in the 60s was more tailored for the kids, and their dogs.

Ours were lucky dogs, those who left their paw prints buried deep beside our own tracks in the 60s. They were our companions and our protectors. And followers of the simple philosophy, that the only things of importance in life were having fun and showing love.

1960s Tukwila was like Sturgis, South Dakota. for the kids. Except instead of being salty, tough bikers revving up our Harleys, we were just schoolkids sporting Schwinn Stingrays with banana seats, ape hangers and sissy bars.

We were just as enamored with the wind in our faces and the joys of freewheeling down the road as the Sons of Anarchy were. We just traveled a bit more slowly.

We treasured our "Choppers" with as much pride as Jax Teller did. And we often raced and challenged each other to perform dazzling stunts on our bikes. We shared the same sense of camaraderie as the real bikers, when we traveled in our packs.

Truly we were, "Looking for adventure, in whatever came our way"

For myself and the guys I rode with, a big part of our trademark cycling etiquette, was that we would have to "peel out" when we took off. Whether we were in a patch of grass, or in the gravel at the curb. And kick up a little rock behind us for effect.

.We never, ever gently applied our brakes to come to an easy stop. Instead, we'd slam the pedal down, lean into a skid, swerving sideways to a dramatic stop, in a little cloud of dust. Lining up right next to your buddy, who had just slid in the same way. Otherwise, you were riding like a "sissy".

Tearing out from my long gravel driveway, I might see my Dad pouring motor oil from the last oil change on the gravel, to keep the dust down. If he did that today, an EPA swat team would be fast on the scene, to cuff him and take him off to prison.

But after passing Dad, Mabel's house was next on the right side of our driveway. In season, I would stop to grab a plum from her tree for my journey. Or maybe stop in to say "Hi" and help her eat her ice cream.

Mabel Shults was the kindly old widow, who lived next door. Mabel was the first person on our block to have a color TV. She would welcome my friends and I in to watch JP Patches, or Captain Puget, while she dished us up a big bowl of Foremost Maple Nut Ice cream. Sometimes even with some homemade cookies. But her color TV was the biggest treat of all.

Pedaling up past the Bergstroms house, the Altmayers lived across the street. They had a couple majestic horse chestnut trees that produced an endless supply of chestnuts for throwing at each other. Or launching way down the block with a bat. The Altmayers also had a horse pasture with a nice slope, that would be our first stop for sledding on a snowy day.

Coming to the end of my street, I could head down 146th to Tukwila Elementary, Tukwila Park and to the marshes that would someday become our huge shopping center, Southcenter.

Or I could head down the long hill on 58th to Interurban Avenue for a Popsicle at Tukwila Store. Continue past our local country western bar, the Riverside Inn, Foster Golf links and eventually reach Seattle.

The point is, there were many directions and many roads to choose from. Which one we chose was just whatever was the fun flavor of the day.

Unbridled, whether alone or with friends, there was a safety and freedom to experience and embrace life, unlike any time since.

For all of us "Baby Boomer" kids, living in the Land of the Hazelnuts was living in a "Boomtown". Landing here in Tukwila of all places, we had hit the jackpot.

2

EVERYBODY'S TALKIN'

Most Tukwila kids were bilingual in the 60s. We spoke traditional English as a second language for our parents, teachers and other adults. But among ourselves, we mostly spoke "COOL"

While out parents reminisced about the "GOOD OLD DAYS", we were living in "RIGHTEOUS" times. Not that our world was filled with righteousness and virtue. Far from it. Being an "altar boy". was not part of being cool

In fact, "BAD: was just beginning to become good. No one was yet, "BAD to the BONE" That didn't evolve until the late 70s. But a little rebelliousness and insolence earned you a lot of "cool points".

Our cool jargon distinguished us from the old people and the uncool. I swear, if you peppered it with a few cuss words, you might even become "HIP" someday.

And if someone said you were "Bitchin'", they weren't saying that you were a "whiner" or complainer. They were complimenting you on just how cool you were!

How we expressed ourselves was one indicator that we part of the "IN CROWD". Certainly, it took more than words to make one "COOL". Are you getting this so far? Or as we would say, "Can you DIG it?"

Contrary to popular belief, no one EVER used the "F" WORD. Absolutely NOT, or "NO WAY" as we would put it. "FAB" was sometimes attributed to 60's lingo, but no one I knew ever said FAB, as a cool abbreviation for FABULOUS.It just wasn't very cool. Maybe it was in Liverpool. But not here in Tukwila, USA.

Or "GROOVY". Unless you were one of the MONKEES, you would stay clear of that one. Groovy made you sound like a "DORK". It was one of those words that the uncool would use when they were trying to be cool, but they really weren't.

I don't know why, but I just can't stand the contemporary greeting that began to become popular in the late 80's or the early 90s and persists today. "WHAT'S UP?" or even worse, "WAZZUP?" just irritates me for some reason.

In our RIGHTEOUS times, instead we would ask, "WHAT'S HAPPENING?"

Somehow to me, it expressed a sincere curiosity and interest in what you've been up to and implied you thought there was something noteworthy and worth inquiring about. It seemed like warm, friendly greeting. It's hard not to smile when asking that.

"WHAT'S UP?" come across as "edgy", curt and cold. It smacks of "What the HELL do YOU want?" or "What's the matter?" Or "Get to the point...I haven't got all day".

What's happening though, was a cool way to greet someone. But what was even cooler, was to translate it into Spanish and dip it in a hit of a Mexican accent, asking "Que Pasa?"

Right away you knew you were speaking to someone who was incredibly cool, and you were glad to share "What's Up" with them. It was groovy....

But "COOL" wasn't the ultimate flattery. Some things were so cool, that they would bubble out of the cool pool, and go "FAR OUT". man. Occasionally something would even surpass far out, and would become, "OUT of SIGHT"

Out of Sight was so cool, that they couldn't even be touched or seen anymore. The epitome of coolness.

There were "DUDES" and "DUDETTES", but they didn't live in Tukwila. They lived on a ranch someplace. Maybe even as close as Kent or Auburn. But we didn't use those "hick" references in the land of cool.

If you were a cool guy, they'd call you "MAN", not a dude. And we called cool girls "CHICKS", not "dudettes"

But the suffix "Man" wasn't just limited to the masculine.It was so commonly tacked on to our conversation that it often crossed over the gender lines. Long before anyone had "crossed over" the gender lines.

We even tried to use it across generational lines. It didn't always go over well.

Mom- "I told you to clean up your room"

"I don't have time, Man...."

Mom- "Well, FIND time. And I'm NOT a MAN...."

Dad's wouldn't take offense. But they would just bounce your slang expressions back on you, sarcastically.

Dad- "Go mow the lawn"

"Oh, come on Man....I just mowed it last week...."

Dad- "And now it's time to mow it again....'MAN'...."

Man! That was NOT Cool!

To their faces, you always called them "Mom" and "Dad". But to be cool around your friends, you might refer to them as the "Old man" or "Old lady" But don't let your old man hear you say it...

If you were in trouble, your parents would often address you with your full, first, middle and last name. As though you were being sworn in on the stand. Getting called by your "court name", let you know they were very serious about what they were saying to you.

I suppose some of the more stuffy, rich, refined kids might have referred to their Mom and Dad as "Mother" and "Father".

But in my world, it was cool for the kids to stick with Mom and Dad. I think once in a while when daughters wanted to take the tone of their communication to the next level, they would change their salutations to an emphasized "MOTHER...."

But as a guy, I never did that, nor did any of my friends.

I understand in England, they referred to women or girls as "Birds". Calling them birds, just didn't fly here in the states. In the slang world, you might be "FLIPPIN' someone the BIRD", which meant giving them the "finger". But in this part of America at least, if you called a "chick" a "bird", they would think that you were "Cuckoo".

I don't recall hearing anyone ask to "Give me FIVE" in the early days of cool either.

It was more common as you held out your hand for a good slappin', and tell them to, give you "SOME SKIN".

Certainly, there were no "HIGH Fives" They hadn't been invented yet. We kept our skin exchanges low in the early 60s.

Oddly, "SKINS" were also another way to say dollars. And if someone had said, "Let's do the WAVE" at a sporting event, we would have probably been just waving our hands at the players on the field.

There was no "HIP HOP" back then. There was HIP and there was HOP, with no connection between the two. Hip was ultra-cool. And hop meant to hurry, like to "HOP to IT". And if you were going someplace, you didn't say it was time to "Go".

No, instead, it was time to "BOOGIE". If you were in a BIG hurry, you'd say, "I've got to BOOK".

It didn't matter if you were on foot, a bicycle or in a car. You didn't need a PICK-UP truck to be "TRUCKIN'". "

"Gotta get Truckin", just meant you had to get on the move. And to encourage someone to keep going in the direction they were heading, you'd tell them to "Keep on Truckin'".

In my youth, there was a big bounty on being "cool". It affected your popularity, and that acceptance enhanced the quality of your life.

A whole new, "Counterculture" was emerging, traditions were being challenged on many fronts. If your language or behavior was perceived as being "Old Fashioned", or "Corny" then you might be tagged as a "Square".

To be branded as a Square was a death sentence socially. Most kids strived to be cool. Many of us would sacrifice what we knew to be "Right" for what was "Hip".

I'm not justifying it, I'm just "Telling it like it Is"

Ironically, the mantra of the decade was "Do your Own Thing". Don't conform to the old fashioned "norms" of society, but instead to

20

make your own "normal". Doing that would make you "cool" according to the theory.

It was a catchy slogan but doing your own thing DIDN'T make anyone cool. Unless, "Your Own Thing" coincided with what was everybody who was cool was doing.

A better formula for cool was to embrace all the styles, vernacular and attitudes of the new "Pepsi Generation" rather than the stale, contrasting ways of the "Establishment"

Defining what was cool came not only from your friends, but from the music you listened to, from your older siblings, and from TV.

Coolness was "Doubling your Pleasure" with Double Mint Gum. or making "Things go Better" with Coca Cola.

Commercials suggested that if you did what was cool, you'd probably end up with a pretty chick having a "blast".

Fact or fable, we young "sponges" soaked it up, thirstily.

Your friends would set the bar for the proper amount of conformity and/or rebellion you needed to be a card carrying "cool guy". Peer pressure had the impact and force of a nuclear bomb on a kid.

A accusation that you were a "chicken" would have you fleeing the coop of common sense to try something that was stupid. but brave. Courage meant more than smarts. Wisdom seemed vastly overrated in the shadow of peer acceptance.

They weren't always amicable relationships, but older brothers were experts on what was cool. My older brother Tom and his friends demonstrated the next level of "Cool", which was far cooler than "grade school" cool.

Tom, Mike's brother Joe Bergstrom and Howard Harrison were roughly from the same time frame as me. But being a few years older, they were more experienced and worldly than either myself. or my own friends.

Tom knew cool. But to our big brothers, few things are less cool than your little brother is. With each two steps I'd take forward in becoming an "Outta Sight" guy, I'd have to take a step or two backwards after getting a "Get Outta here, you little Squirt" rebuke from Tom

He knew as well as I did, that I would never become as cool as he was. At least until I got older.

I wasn't alone. It was known and accepted among all of us younger siblings, that our brothers were a few grades ahead of us in "class", and a few steps ahead of us in "hipness"

Still, many of us looked up to the older kids as role models, for good or bad. We were all just sorting things out in our childhoods.

Hopefully, by the time we were ready to leave our comfort zone of Tukwila and venture out into the real world, we would have kept only the good and worthy values from our mentors that made us cool. And tossed away the "cool" garbage.

Discovering how to combine that good "cool" with our uniqueness that defines who we are, would put us well on our way to "Doing our Own Thing"

If we succeeded, we would have truly become, "Cool, Man".

And, it wouldn't that be "Outta Sight"?

3

ANTI-DEPRESSION

"You kids just don't know how good you have it" Dad would say. Sure, we did. You reminded us of it all the time.

You grew up in the depression and walked 5 miles to and from school. uphill in both directions. After chopping your daily cord of wood, or course. You had nothing to eat but beans, for breakfast, lunch and dinner. And then you would be punished when you farted. I know times were tough then. But I also believe you exaggerated a little.

Your only Christmas present was a single candy cane. Which they would have to split six ways. But you felt grateful that you had gotten anything at all. You only got to go to the movies once a year, and it was black and white.

After struggling to make it at home, you were then sent off to war in Europe or the South Pacific. Good luck was not winning the lottery, but just the good fortune to make it home alive.

Then you started your family and got locked into a mortgage that required you to work long hard hours in a sweaty factory. Meanwhile, Mom worked from sunrise to sunset to feed the kids in a spotless, comfortable home.

You did it all for us. Of course, we were grateful and thankful for all the sacrifices you made.

But as you said, you did it to give your children a better life than you had. So, we were determined to have a better time than you did. And we did our best to do just that.

"Where do you think you're going?" Dad demanded

"Out to play with my friends" I replied

"Not until you mow that LAWN, Sport...." he would growl

With a heavy sigh and a moan kept under my breath, I'd head out to the shed to grab the mower, and pull the start cord a dozen times trying to get it to fire up.

Even after that, sometimes it wouldn't start. But our Dads back then could fix anything...with our help.

They would dismantle it and get a coffee can of gasoline for soaking the offending parts in. With a cigarette dangling from their mouths about a foot or two from the flammable fumes.

Our job was to hand him tools and keep his cigarette going.

Washing the parts in gas with bare hands, his cigarette ash would fall in the can. Before we both ignited into a glorious fireball, he would hand you his cigarette for safekeeping.

While you winced at the noxious smoke burning your eyes he would do his repair magic. Then in a minute, he'd have the mower running like a top.

When you were in trouble, Dad might "Hand you your butt". But after he successfully fixed the lawn mower, you would hand him back his own butt.

Chores were just a part of the harsh reality of life for most kids.

Girls would often be tasked with doing dishes or vacuuming or other housework.

Boys did jobs like taking out the trash or mowing the lawn. I loved having a big yard to play in, but at mowing time, I sometimes wished that we lived in an apartment.

But today, there would be no mower rebuild in a cloud of tobacco smoke. It was just being stubbornly hard to start.

"You FLOODED it..."

"Let her sit for a few minutes!" Dad yelled out the window cracking a can of Lucky Lager beer with a church key. Beer pull tabs had yet to be invented.

Rolling my eyes, I'd continue muttering about the injustices of life as I stomped on the molehills while waiting for the gas to evaporate from the mower.

Shamrock, our dog was sniffing in the grass for a garter snake. Grasshoppers would sail by my face, occasionally poking me in the eye on their impressive leaps.

Tukwila was almost as famous for Dandelions as it was for Hazelnuts and by midsummer mowing were more pruning the tops off the yellow blooms than mowing actual grass.

I cursed our yard for being so big, while being thankful for the blackberries that covered about 3/4 of our intimidating 3 acre spread.

I believed that blackberries were a communist plot to take over America from within. You could actually watch them grow a couple inches in the time it took for a lawn mower to un-flood. But for kids like me, the Russians had done us a big favor. Less lawn to mow.... more time to play.

Resuming my mowing, I saw my best friend, Lon Shankel coming up the hill from the Bergstroms horse pasture, next door emerging from the tall hay.

I think it was in first grade when I first met Lon Shankel. The kids had all called him Lon Mower, and being so gullible, I fell for it. When I told my Mom, my new buddy's name, she laughed.

"Honey, are you sure?   I can't imagine any parents named Moore, who would their son, Lon...."

"Oh yeah... That's his name!" I replied authoritatively. Then, as it is now, sometimes my imagination would accidentally enhance my stories a bit.

"Even the teacher calls him Lon Moore"

I actually believed that I had heard our teacher call him Lon Mower with a straight face in roll call.   But when Lon met my Mom, we all laughed when he corrected us and told us his surname was actually Shankel.

Over the roar of the mower, he shouted, "Come on, Ed....Let's get going"

I shut off the mower.

"I can't. My Dad nabbed me on the way out the door. Told me that I've got to get all this grass mowed before I can go anywhere"

"I know how it is..." 'Shank" said as he started to play tug of war with the garter snake that Shamrock had been swinging around like a whip. "My Dad made me help in the garden before he let me go"

"Yeah...it's just not right" I complained. "You know, here it is summer, and we're supposed to be kids. We shouldn't have to work. We're supposed to be having fun. Everybody else is. And I have to do all this for a measly $5.00 allowance".

"What are you whining about? I had to feed our rabbits, weed the vegetables and wash his car, and Dad doesn't give me a dime"

"Yeah, but you got your paper route..."

"Come on. Hurry up and finish up so we can go..."

I fired up the mower and then stalled it as the blades got caught in the carcass of Shamrock's mangled snake.

"Look out, I'll get it" Lon said as unfurled the bloody, headless snake from the mower blades. Then he yanked the pull start and started to mow the last patches of the yellow blooms.

A stray rock made a perfect line drive and sent it blasting right through our kitchen window. A mole popped his head out of his hole, startled by the clamor. Dad's head snapped out of the front door angry and agitated, with beer squirting out of the crushed can in his clenched fist....

"How many times have I TOLD you to make sure you pick up the rocks before you start mowing?" Realizing it was merely a rhetorical question, I thought it better not to answer, and decided to look down at my feet remorsefully, instead.

"There went your allowance, young fella" he scoffed as he headed into the house to call the neighborhood handyman Al Hemick to fix it.

"Not again" I complained to Shank, shaking my head.

"Yeah, don't worry. I've still got some money left from my route. Let's 'book'," he said.

Lon was the most generous guy in the world. Once in a while, I'd help him with his paper route. But whether or not I did, he would always have money and make sure we had our required daily allowance of candy from Frank's Fixit Shop, or Tukwila grocery.

Today was hot, so rather than do the half mile climb from the Tukwila store, we chose to pedal our stingrays down the easier grade to Franks.

Frank would always be in the back bringing lawn mowers back from the dead after kids had ruined them by mowing snakes and rocks,

His wife, "Mrs. Fixit" would be at the candy counter. Even if you only had some loose change in your pocket, you could buy a lot of sugar, as they had a number of penny candies that were brimming with life energizing carbs.

For a dime you could get a Baby Ruth that was as big as a D cell flashlight. Located at the base of that formidable mountain, "Bremmer's Hill", Frank's Fixit Shop made a fortune fueling school kids with candy to make the strenuous climb uphill to Showalter each morning during the school year.

But even in the summertime, we needed to stop in to maintain our well rooted addictions to the sweets. Especially if you had a paper route.

4

BRINGING YOU THE NEWS

It wasn't fair. All the other kids were having a regular "hay day", riding down the long stalks of beaten down dried grass on cardboard sheets on "Sliding Hill", just behind the paper shack on Fifty Sixth Street.

One of many wide open, undeveloped spaces around Tukwila, Sliding Hill was invented by some visionary kid who had noticed the matted down straw made a rather slick surface perfect for "tobogganing" over the knolls of the slope on a hot summer day.

It offered all the thrills, but none of the chills of winter sledding. Sliding Hill was just another home brewed flavor of summer fun that we had invented.

On another day, we would be right with them, joining in the good times, but amid the yelling and laughter taunting us from over the hill., we were stuck working. Stuffing the advertising supplements in a big stack of Wednesday papers, with a long paper route still waiting to be delivered

While it did seem unjust that we were slaving away and missing out on the sliding action, theoretically we would be the happy kids with a few bucks in our pockets to spend on goodies at Frank's Fixit, or the Tukwila Store. Honestly though, we would have rather had it both ways with time for fun in our day AND a jingle in our pockets.

Lon had an easy route. It was comprised mostly of all the apartments along Macadam Road and above the Southcenter Shopping Center. With an apartment paper route and a decent throwing arm, you could use "air mail" to deliver most of your papers without doing as much traveling.

Throwing blind up to the second and third level hallways, I'm sure he had whacked quite a few of his customers who would dare step outside at delivery time. And he had startled quite a few others.

As Tukwila grew, slowly more and more romping grounds for children were being replaced by sprawling apartment complexes. It was sad for the kids, but happy news for the paperboys. Replacing houses with apartments would turn our paper routes in "Gravy Trains".

Before Lon had his, I once worked a Seattle Times route too. But I made my money the hard way. I worked the mean streets of 56th, 57th and 58th where the houses were far apart, and the driveways were steep and long. In addition, it was all hills. For me, the token neighborhood Fat Kid, it was "The Hill Street Blues"

I actually didn't make money. I was paying off the debts on my dream bike.

It was the age of the "Stingrays", and to kids our bikes were like our "Orange County Choppers". It wasn't a Schwinn, but when my eyes saw the Sear's "Spyder" painted bright gold, with the tiger striped seat, I drooled. I was rabid about getting it.

My folks had already bought me an old fashioned "cruiser" bike, but it really wasn't cool enough for the "club". I'd had this same "square" bike since I started riding with "training wheels". That wasn't right! It was like riding a Honda 90 in the a motorcycle gang. Frugal Mom and Dad surely gave us everything we needed but were unlikely to shell out just to keep me on the cutting edge of "coolness".

So Tom became my banker. .

My brother Tom was the "Station Manager" at the paper shack, and he had wearied of doing his route. The station manager's job was to take the papers that came in on the truck, count them and set them out for the carriers to deliver.

An easy, well-paying job, it was a sweet gig for him. But to be station manager, you had to have a route. So in exchange for a loan on my bike with undefined terms, he subcontracted his route to me and kept the gravy and prestige of Station Manager. My paycheck? I was riding on it.

I've never been very business savvy, but it seems like I worked a long, long time to pay for that bike. To be fair, my wages would have had to be adjusted for "delivery errors" when my picky customers weren't happy about getting wet papers or no papers at all.

Listen, I was a chubby little boy, and on a hot day climbing to the top of 144th might have caused a heat stroke or at least brought me serious fatigue. So, a couple houses way up there, may not get the daily paper each and every day.

And whether it was a slow news day or not, that Seattle Times press kept rolling. So, for 6 days a week every afternoon, and at the sick hour of 6am on Sundays, I was expected to deliver. There should have been child labor laws.

Sometimes on a rainy day, I would conserve energy by tossing the paper in the middle of the yard instead of on your protected porch. Is that any reason to call the paper and complain? All they had to do would be to put it by the furnace vent and it should be ready to read in a week or so. Instead those "whiners" would rather ruin my reputation.

If that wasn't enough to crush a kid's head...a Country Squire station wagon could do the trick. I almost gave my to bring people their papers one day...

I was riding down 56th street with my paper sack slung around my neck, and I started to turn left to deliver the Woyvoditches paper. Jeff Moore's Mom had been driving behind me as I slowly pedaled. She moved over to the left to pass me.

Just as I started to make my own turn without looking, my handlebars struck the door of her station wagon, and my bike went down. Flying over the handlebars of my tumbling bike, I skidded on my face to a stop with my head about an inch and a half away from her front right tire. Rolled up papers surrounded my sprawled-out body, like chalk lines at a murder scene.

Mrs. Moore was frantic, leaping out to check on my apparent corpse lying in the street. I was okay. More importantly, so was my beautiful Spyder bike. But she felt awfully bad about it just the same.

It wasn't really her fault. She had signaled and done everything a driver was supposed to do. She couldn't help it if I had carelessly turned into her car. But, having kids of her own, I'm sure she knew. Unlike cats who have only 9, kids had unlimited lives.

Bicycle crashes were just another small part of the daily grind of childhood. What should have been deadly falls from tree branches were commonplace. The same falls would at the very least paralyze us if we suffered them today in our 60s, if not send us to the funeral home. But we couldn't count the times that we got the wind knocked out of ourselves doing so as kids. And returned to fall again another day.

We were often impaled by nails in our feet. Yet we suffered no amputations from gangrene. Smacked in the head by stepped on rakes frequently, it's never been proven that any of us received any traumatic brain injuries. Suspected, but unproven.

Band aids and Bactine were the jewelry and cologne that we wore in our youth. There was no injured reserve list for kids. We just limped and bleed through another day of fun.

Rather than a cool Stingray type bike, Lon's was a boxy utility bike built for paper routes. Big and sturdy, it had dual baskets on the back and he could load it up with hundreds of papers in the baskets. Then he would add his loaded paper sacks on top of it.He had a huge route for a kid.

When I'd tag along on his route, it was mostly to keep him company. He had the great throwing guns for hitting the higher up apartments, but occasionally he'd ask me to deliver a few of the low-level units for him.

But in mid-July, after finishing Lon's route, there was plenty of time before sunset to swing by Harrison's Pond. But of course, I had to check in at home first.

We'd spend pretty much all day everyday out and about. But if you didn't check in at the agreed upon times, you would find yourself on restriction and lose your freedoms. It was kind of like being on parole all the time.

The sun was blazing when we returned to my house, with empty paper sacks and a powerful thirst. It wasn't often when he did it, but that day Dad was just getting ready to drive up and get some refreshment for us all. We rode along. With Dad up to the A&W.

Hardly anyone had air conditioning back then, but the next best thing was having all the windows down, and the wing vents diverting a steady stream of warm, albeit moving wind into our faces.

Dad always said regarding Air Conditioning, "It's just one more thing to break down". If they didn't have something back in the depression, it was a hard sell to convince him we needed it here in the jet age.

A series of turns brought us past the paper station and sliding hill. Then down Gott's Hill, past Pamco Crankshaft and Frank's Fixit Shop. Passing Spencer Pottery, the car would have to downshift to make it up steep, Bremmer's Hill.

Driving beyond Showalter elementary we'd pass the famous rock painted with the ruling classes graduation year at Foster High. This rock probably was once but a pebble, but after millions of coats of paint from every class that ever-attended Foster, it had become a boulder.

As we hit Highway 99, we were drawing near. Our mouths watered like sprinklers with thirst.

It would have been even cooler a decade before when the car lot was filled with 57 Chevys and carhops skated over with your orders. But it was still an oasis in the summer heat.

The car hops didn't skate out anymore as they had in the 1950s, but the cars still pulled up to the curb and ordered through the same microphones. Soon the girls, sporting saddle shoes rather than roller skates, would bring your order out to you in a tray that would hang out the driver's window,.

Everyone has had Root Beer from a bottle or can, but you haven't had real Root Beer unless you had it straight from the keg at the A&W or Triple X. In a frosted mug, it was instant relief from the summer heat. It just isn't the same today drinking the CO_2 and syrup mixed in a fountain and poured into a waxed paper cup. It was a "gas" to drink it from the frozen glass.

You'd have to go back in a time machine to taste the difference, but believe me, if you missed the 60s and 70s, you've never REALLY had a root beer. A float with a big scoop of ice cream was even better. But that treat was reserved for those rare days when the mercury rose up into the 90s.

Sometimes Dad might buy a gallon in a frozen glass jug to take home. It was a bona fide, wide mouthed, thick walled jug with a little thumb handle on the side. Just like the ones the Hillbillies used in their jug bands.

The nice thing about a gallon was you got some root beer for now, and more for later. We would pour from the gallon jug right into our own frosted mugs that we had bought from A&W on a previous visit. Maybe enjoy a slice of watermelon along with the root beer and spit the seeds that will never grow around here, in the yard.

Refreshed, Lon and I would park our bikes, and walk a well beaten path through Mabel's woods up to Harrison's pond.

5

HARRISON'S POND

It was the closest thing that we had to a lake in our immediate neighborhood. With Lilly pads, pussy willows and cat tails jutting out of the slimy, algae green water. No fish were swimming in the mucky waters. They probably would have died. But the pond was thick with Salamanders and Frogs.

I don't know if they were leeches or tadpoles, but there was a huge colony of tiny, sperm cellish creatures squirming around the shores. Water skippers would dance between the Lilly pads, as the crickets and frogs chirped and croaked. Isolated by woods, it was a nice peaceful little getaway where you could commune with nature, at least up to your knees while you searched for your new amphibious pet.

Salamanders ranged in color from a dark tan to a deep brown, so they were sometimes hard to pick out in the murky water. But we could always capture a couple of them, after a desperate slippery struggle. And they would become our reluctant, new take home buddies.

But our companionship would be short lived. Just like our memories were.

The frogs and salamanders we would capture would be placed in an old pickle jar that we had selected especially for them

We thoughtfully and considerately remembered to punch holes in the lids with a nail, so they could breathe, and made sure they had some water and a little vegetation in their transparent homes for their amusement and nutrition.

Then we would take them home and leave them to sunbathe by the side of the house as we took off on our next adventure.

It wasn't deliberate cruelty, but rather an unintentional neglect. Kids were scatterbrained and became distracted easily. But we would usually come across the putrid remains of our pets a couple weeks later, dry and dead with wilted blades of grass draping their carcasses. I feel bad about it now, but we didn't think much of it at the time.

Harrison's pond had a little makeshift wooden raft, probably made by kids a generation or two prior to our visits. Lon and I would take the nearly waterlogged craft from one side to the other on each trip to the pond. As Tom Sawyer and Huck Finn had done a century before on the "Mighty Missisip"

One day Lon had what seemed like a great idea at the time for floating something different.

"Hey Ed....Why don't you take off your shoes, and we'll float them around like little boats?"

"Yeah, okay" I agreed. My new Hush Puppies looked like quite seaworthy ships to me.

The pups were buoyant, and they sailed pretty good, for a while. We pushed them around the drink, pants rolled up to our knees. But soon they were beginning to take on water through the lace holes and seams.

It was kind of interesting watching them slowly turn into little submarines sinking, little by little. But eventually one of the shoes got away from us and headed out to the unknown depths of the middle of the pond. And of course, descended to the bottom of the little sea.

The water was filthy, and the scummy mud and weeds wrapped around our calves as we frantically searched for my fairly new oxfords. It would have taken a team of trained divers a long time to find my shoe, which probably became a sanctuary for salamanders fleeing from the little boys trying to imprison them.

Mom and Dad were not very understanding when I returned home with only one shoe instead of a pair.

"What were you thinking? I just bought you those shoes from the Wigwam, not two weeks ago! Whatever possessed you to do that?" Mom asked.

"Well, Lon thought they would float" I explained, throwing my friend under the bus. After all he wasn't going to get in trouble. I thought deflecting the blame might help.

"Really? Well, why didn't Lon use HIS shoes for boats then?"

It was a valid question that I hadn't considered up until then.

"I don't know. We didn't think of that...." I replied honestly.

In Seattle in the winter it sometimes got into freezing temperatures, but we were not known for the deep freezes that are experienced in other parts of the country.

On one chilly morning, Dad asked me, "Where are you going?"

"I'm going up to Harrison's pond. Its frozen over right now"

"Hey, don't you be walking out on the ice...you don't know how thick it is..."

"Okay" I answered as I walked out the door.

I think both he and I knew that once I got there I would be testing the waters. I mean why else would I want to go to the pond on an icy day?

But it was his fatherly duty to warn me of the danger regardless of the fact that he knew I would surely blow off his wise advice.

Still, his words resonated in my ears as I approached the iced-up shores. I really didn't know how thick the ice was. So, I tread carefully. Knowing the pond pretty well, while I didn't know the thickness of the ice, I did know how deep the pond was unfrozen in various spots around the perimeter. So, I walked out a couple feet, and gave it a good stomp.

"Seems pretty sturdy" I thought. I skated around a bit in my boots near the shoreline. It seemed thick enough. I went out a few more feet and tested it again with a full two-legged jump.

No cracks, so I frolicked a bit more on the glassy surface. After skating with my shoes at the shoreline, I ventured out a few more feet.

CRACK...I didn't even have to jump on the ice. A fracture line stretched across the pond and before I could scramble toward the shore, my two feet sunk about two feet through to the icy water. The instant chill was alarming and triggered my adrenaline. Pulling my feet out, I nearly tripped and made it even harder to break away from the jagged edges of the ice. Lesson learned.

I returned home with my feet and shoes cold, numb and drenched in ice cold socks. I sneaked in and warmed my feet then changed my socks and shoes without my Dad knowing about my disobedience and misfortune.

But I really was thankful for his warning. Without it, I might have strutted right out into the deep part. And fallen in over my head. Maybe they would have found me weeks later, cryogenically preserved and reunited with my lost shoe.

For High School Biology years later, Harrison's pond was a lush petri dish for collecting samples to examine under the microscope. Seeing the Burchard Gardens of Bacteria. Amoeba and Algae, squirming infectiously around on our microscope slides made us wonder how we ever survived splashing around in that muck in our younger days.

What was once Harrison's pond now sits surrounded by another enormous apartment complex. But if the people living inside those units knew of all the fun and memories those waters had seen, they would probably smile too.

Near Harrison's pond was an abandoned old farmhouse with dilapidated barns and chicken houses. It was fun to explore the rickety old structures. And it was a goldmine for finding wood to build our camps and tree houses.

Sometimes it was a little bit spooky wandering around in the semi darkness and the boards would creak eerily as we walked across them.

We weren't the first kids to cannibalize these buildings and there were lots of missing planks and rejected ones left with nails sticking up strewn about the ruins.

More than once, I had impaled my foot with one of those rusty nails and to this day, I cringe when I think of the sensation of the steel plunging inches into my heel.

And as though getting stabbed in the foot wasn't bad enough, your parents would take you off to the doctor to get poked a second time with a tetanus shot.

As bad as that was, the alternative you were told, was to not treat the insult, and come down with lockjaw. And never be able to speak or eat again. As our local fat kid, I could probably live without the talking, but no more eating? Just shoot me and put me out of my misery.

Around Puget Sound, water was everywhere. More days than not, our air was filled with rain. Drainage ditches became little rivers and the thousands of chuckholes on the crumbling asphalt streets were seasonal lakes all fall, winter and spring. Every kid's foot soles were wrinkled much of the year beneath their soggy socks.

The Duwamish river circles around both the south side and the east side of Tukwila. Lon and I had a little fishing hole right next to where Interurban Boulevard crosses over the river on the south side of town.

We caught mostly bullheads and would toss them back, but occasionally we'd land a cutthroat trout suitable for eating. But it wasn't so much about the catch as it was just hanging out and chewing the fat as the river currents swirled over the lushly vegetated banks.

Our civil engineers have gotten smarter lately with the addition of floodgates on our dams, but in the lowlands around the Dairy Farm in the 60s, sometimes the river banks would put the whole dam thing underwater.

Crossing over Grady Way toward Renton, we would sometimes see the heads of cows popping out of the muddy water. And farmers in rowboats passing out hay to the soaking bovines. I guess the milkers had to be scuba divers at those times.

Further on down the river as the Duwamish traveled toward Puget Sound, the river passed by a tire swing that many kids used to hurl themselves into the middle of the Duwamish on summer days.

It was a little out of my neighborhood, so I never actually ventured down there myself.

Sadly, around 6th or 7th grade in the midst of having fun, my friend Delbert Webster's older brother Jim, had drowned in that spot

Jim was the first kid we knew who had died, and it was inconceivable to all of us that something like this could ever happen to someone our age.

My parents had often mentioned the "undertows" created by sunken logs in the rapids of the river. Jim's passing proved the undertow wasn't just a myth.

For some of the kids who lived in the Duwamish and Riverton neighborhoods, the river flowed with money too, as it rounded the Foster Golf Links.

These enterprising kids would dive for Titleist golf balls that wound up in the drink and then resell them at a steep discount to golfers on the course. Kids discovered religion as they would pray for the golfers to slice.

Real golf fans may love a scratch golfer, but these guys were most fond of the hacks. The worse you could golf, the more these ball diver kids would like you.

They say if you hold a seashell to your ear, you can hear the ocean waves. We didn't have to go any further than Saltwater Park in Des Moines to bring a bit of Puget Sound back home with us.

The sands were littered with seashells as we combed the shores. And hundreds of dollars' worth of sand dollars too. I've been there recently, and I don't see much "money" lying around there anymore.

Where did it all go? Did we pick it dry? You still see a couple :"clams" here and there. But if you're looking for shell, you're better off at the gas station, these days.

And back in the 60s and 70s, you could walk the shores of Saltwater sniffing the perfume of wood fires from the campground at the park. They still have the camping, but they no longer allow campfires. What kind of camping is that? Even Smokey the Bear would disapprove.

All of the Tukwila kids learned to swim at Angle Lake Park, near the Sea Tac Airport.

I remember the Angle Lake's beach being packed with big crowds of people sunbathing with their pocket-sized transistor radios tuned into our top 40 station, KJR, while we were being taught to swim.

First, they taught us how to blow bubbles. Then how to face float in the pristine waters of the lake.

By the time we had graduated to the back float, it was about time to rid ourselves of some of that Kool Aid that we'd been drinking in the summer heat.

The distance to the restrooms was daunting. So, while the teacher was distracted, it wasn't only me, but there were plenty of other little boys who also found relief from our full bladders in the water where we stood. The water suddenly felt a little warmer

Once we finally learned to dog paddle, we took the "dog thing" to the next logical step and would sometimes back ourselves up to the dock and do as Rover might do in your yard.

It was very important to make sure you kept your back to the dock, because a floater would certainly blow your cover.

Yes, the restrooms were quite a hike from the water, but if you needed a drink of water, you'd gladly walk up to the water fountain rather than drinking from those apparently clear blue waters. We knew better than that.

Being the fat kid, gave me the special super power of "buoyancy" in the water. While all the other kids would have to either "sink or swim", fat floats. So, I didn't even have to tread water. My head would always be bobbing above the surface no matter what I did or didn't do with my arms and legs. I was virtually unsinkable.

With all its drawbacks, there were a few benefits from being chubby. For one thing I had an "innie" belly button that resembled like a happy little mouth.

When I would lift my shirt up and suck my gut in, then let it out.... I could make my belly button look like he was blowing out a candle. I got so good at it I could even make it "talk" like a mannequin. My tummy made a pretty good dummy.

I should have drawn a nose and some little eyes above my pie hole.

"Hey Ed. Make him say, 'I'm Fat'How appropriate. No problem.

"Hey Ed, Make him FART...." Buzzing my lips as I puffed my belly cheeks out and blew from my navel mouth earned big belly laughs from the small audience of small people.

It was quite entertaining I was told. I got many requests to perform this hysterical skit, and the exercise kept my belly button pretty much free of lint most of the time, amid the applause. It was strictly for the amusement of the locals, my act never made it to Vegas.

There was also no one better than me to serve as the "anchorman" in a battle of tug of war. In teeter totter, my partner would always be on the upswing unless I sat closer to the fulcrum.

And if I would lean back, I could really give them a swift launch up in the air. In fact, if you ever need a guy to serve as a counterbalance for any reason, I was a handy kid to have around.

6

STARRY, STARRY NIGHTS

No one had a window air conditioner, heat pump, central air, or even a whole house fan in Tukwila in the 60s.

It hardly ever got really hot here, and we all survived the occasional mid 80s or low 90s days using fans to suck (warm) air in through open windows and doors. But usually a cool rainy day was never far away.

The dry summer nights were perfect for my friends and I to lay out sleeping bags on the grass and dandelions to sleep under the stars.

While our dogs would be on high alert, doing the graveyard watchdog shift, and we would discuss everything under the moon, with the chirping of crickets providing the background music.

Breaking up the conversation now and then with an arm wrestling contest or a game of rock, paper, scissors, we'd talk until the wee hours of the morning.

There was no texting, the only technology we brought was perhaps a tinny transistor radio playing songs like "Summer in the City" until the batteries finally gave out.

Spit bugs would be casting their loogies on the clover as swarms of mosquitoes hovered over us. hungry for a midnight snack.

To demonstrate our machismo, we would welcome mosquitoes landing on our arms. And fearlessly gawk at them drilling with their Proboscises into our skin.

We'd watch them pulling our blood through their pipeline and see their bodies glow red before mashing them into a blotch of their blood and our own on our flesh. At least we let them enjoy their "last supper" before executing them for their bloody assault.

I also remember having slugging contests. No not in the face, but on one another's biceps. Just to prove how "tough" we were.

You'd have to grin and bear the other guy pounding his fist on your arm without flinching, or risk being called a "sissy".

My buddy Lon liked to take the contest to the next level, playing a game he invented and called, "Bloody Knuckles"

Taking turns holding out our fists while the other would slam them with their own. The first one who drew blood won the contest. I didn't really like that game, but you know, we little boys had to play it, to prove our "manliness"

We all start out in our lives with empty brains. And like sponges we all suck up information and begin to formulate our thoughts and opinions from day one. But especially as kids, our cognitive realm is virgin soil. We don't know what we think, until we've thought it and seen if it makes sense.

Gazing up into the endless skies on a clear summer night is the perfect setting for philosophical meanderings. In the still of the night deep thoughts would be shared among good friends.

Contemplating the boundaries of space was a frequent puzzle we would explore. How many stars were there? Where is the wall where the universe stops? Or does it just keep going forever? How could it stop and there be nothing beyond it? But equally perplexing, how could it go on forever?

What about our own existence? We couldn't' remember a time of when we weren't around. Yet we knew we had once not been. We couldn't digest our own beginnings or contemplate our eventual endings.

What would start as an interesting pondering of the concepts of infinity would suddenly turn disturbing as we recognized the impossibility of solving these mysteries. Until someone would say, "This is freaking me out.... Let's talk about something else"

Small talk would seem trivial after tackling such enormous matters as the cosmos and our place in it. These mysteries were far bigger than our collective minds could fathom.

And soon we would be silent, trying to sleep as the dew began to set on the lawn. Wide eyes staring up at the stars, bewildered by our own smallness and ignorance of a world we may never understand. "Help Mr. Wizard....I don't want to be a philosopher anymore!"

So it was good to corral our conversation into tangible topics. Our interests, our lives and our dreams. Telling jokes, sometime dirty ones that I might not understand, but I would have to at laugh heartily, as though I did.

Posturing was of the utmost importance. You had to pretend like you knew more than you did. There was a huge gap in social standing between a kid who was 8, 8 and a half or 9 years old. Those extra months of experience meant a lot when you haven't really been around that long.

Sometimes, the conversation would turn to girls

7

CHICKS

My first infatuation was Cindy Isler. At five years old, there weren't many girls in my neighborhood to choose from But since the Islers lived across Bergstroms field, right next door to my buddy Jeff Moore, I was drawn to her cute blonde pixie hairdo, and the geographical convenience.

Even as a kindergartner, I was a sucker for those blondes. I even told my Mom that I intended to marry Cindy. As I moved into first grade and beyond, I forgot all about those wedding plans, and noticed there was a smorgasbord of other potential mates in my class. But by the time I hit the third grade, I'd moved on to older women.

My third-grade teacher and heartthrob, Mrs. Rapp was married, but as some of my friends came from divorced homes, I optimistically hoped things might not work out with Mr. Rapp.

But far from stealing the headlines as Teacher Mary Kay Letourneau would years later in a relationship with her 10-year-old student, I was just a apple polishing wannabe, who kept my "Mrs. Rapp sure is pretty" thoughts to myself. As far as I know, the Rapps continued in marital bliss. Oh well, she wasn't a blonde anyway.

Honestly, as our school's token fat kid, I doubt that I even made a footnote in any elementary school girl's diary. And if there was a dream stuffed away in their hope chests regarding me, I think it was "I hope that little Eddy doesn't try to flirt with me".

In the vernacular of early grade school boys, you never used the word "Love' to describe how you felt about girls. The Monkees had a song, "I wanna be Free" in which Davy Jones sang`;

"Don't say you love me, say you LIKE me"

And at a certain point in life when it became kosher to confess you had attractions to the opposite sex, you could admit you "Liked" someone. But if you expressed it in more flowery terms beyond that, the teasing would become ruthless.

"Two little lovers, sitting in a tree, K. I. S. S. I. N. G. First comes love, then comes marriage, then comes baby in the baby carriage', was the anthem of ridicule, that you never wanted to hear sung to you.

Or even worse, they'd pass the word of your crush around school. Then, from a dozen different mouths throughout the day you'd be hearing, "Ed loves So and So" followed by laughter and mocking pantomimed "Kissy Faces" with big exaggerated puckered lips. Still as the song goes, "Everybody 'likes' Somebody, Sometime" And everyone liked to be liked too.

I think for the fat kids like me, the comedy was exaggerated because we were among the least likely to be liked. Not that I was disliked. Girls just didn't "like" me," Like That" I just wasn't the kind of kid that anyone took seriously. Especially girls.

I was often teased. I think I was a ready source of laughter for everyone. It wasn't really too bad. Kids can be cruel, but try as they would, it mostly bounced right off me.

The problem for my "would be" tormentors was that, to me if it was funny, it was funny. I'd laugh just as hard at a fat joke as the one who was taking the stab at me would. I guess I didn't take myself any more seriously than they did.

But in the springtime of the Fifth grade, as the Beach Boys were singing, "I wish they all could be California Girls" on the radio, a pretty, sweet girl with long flowing hair had just immigrated from L.A., along with our local robins returning from their own winter trips to California.

Although I was painfully shy, I was enamored with this picture perfect, California beach blonde who just moved in on the next block. And whether it was out of pity, or friendliness, I could have sworn I saw her throw some rather encouraging smiles my direction.

I might have been the big man on our campus, but that was in girth not my vertical stature. "Sweet talking" her would have sounded ridiculous from this chubby, bashful boy. So, I figured the best way to impress her was with my extraordinary skills on my bike.

I had recently learned how to do a "Wheelie" on my shiny, new Sears Spyder bike, with its tiger seat and the ape hanger handlebars. So, while her spotlight was shining on me, I got it up on my back wheel and did a good ten-foot patch with my front forks hanging proudly high in the air for her.

Her face lit up.   The butterflies fluttered in the Spring air. Maybe she was just giggling at my efforts to impress her. But in my mind's eye I was seeing imaginary little pink hearts floating around her beautiful sun-bleached hair.

My shy grin acknowledged the amused applause in her eyes. It was unspoken, but my raised eyebrows suggested my response. "Hey baby.... Pretty impressive, huh?"

But the best was yet to come. Surely the most surefire stunt to steal a young girl's heart would be the daring, "Look Ma...No Hands" trick, I thought. A flock of Robins began to circle overhead to witness this amazing spectacle. This trick would be sure to "blow her mind, I had hoped.

I'd imagined that in her eyes, I was going to look like Evel Knievel flying his motorcycle over a dozen cars, then through his hoop of flames.

But unlike the daredevil in his red, white and blue superhero costume, I didn't care about getting a standing ovation from the hundreds of adoring fans. I was only looking for the recognition and adoration from that one cute girl.

Sure enough, this mesmerized beauty seemed entranced by my heroic display of talent and balance, as I smugly folded my arms across my chest and pedaled on by her with a beaming smile. "Look at me, I got my Mojo workin' here Honey!"

She might have even rewarded me with an amazed, "Wow" or some soft mock hand clapping at this feat. Maybe the response was exaggerated in my own imagination by my success at capturing her attention. But my chest was swelling proudly at my graduation from a loser, to a player.

As the Spring flowers bloomed colorfully in the yards, I continued to perform for this lucky girl. Cupid's bow was cocked and ready to fire. The birds were dancing with love in the sky above me.

The word must have gotten around the air about me being the fat kid who could take a joke, because one of the birds gave me his sarcastic review of my performance, with a perfectly timed release of bird poop.

He plastered me good on the top of my head. Then he swung back by and dropped me a second load as an ovation, that splattered my right pedaling leg on the upstroke.

Making a girl laugh is of course, a good thing, but it's much better and more attractive when it's not because you're plastered, either with booze, or pooze.

Well, I nervously chuckled too, and probably said something corny like, "Gotta watch out for those low flying birds" before I turned and burnt a little rubber pedaling my embarrassed tail home to clean up.

It wasn't the first time, and certainly wouldn't be the last that I'd play a laughingstock. But whether she thought I was cool or a fool, I just couldn't get her sunny smile out of my mind.

So, in the summertime, as the mosquitoes swarmed on one of many nights in sleeping bags under the warm open skies, I opened up my heart to my friends.

Mike Bergstrom and Punky Summers were both upperclassmen, and as sixth graders they were a little more worldly and sophisticated than myself. They were both familiar with my dream girl, but they listened patiently as I described my fascination with my her, including my bike, bird and shit show story.

"So, you really LIKE her then?" Mike asked.

"Well YEAH..." I admitted, annoyed at the need for a question to validate such an obvious attraction.

"So, what are you going to do about it?" Punky probed.

"Do? I don't know. What am I supposed to do about it?" I asked naively.

"If you really like her, you have to buy her a ring...."

"A ring?" I gasped. "I don't want to marry her...."

They both laughed, "No, a friendship ring"

I'd never heard of such a thing. "Then what?"

"You give it to her" Mike said, amazed at my innocence and ignorance.

"What if she doesn't want it from me...?" I worried.

"Then you take it back and say, 'Well then. If I can't have you... I'll just throw it away'. Then you hold it in your hand and get ready to toss it into the bushes. When she thinks you're going to actually throw the ring, she'll say 'Nooooo!'. And she'll break down and take the ring from you. Then, you're going steady" Punky explained with confidence.

As the guys changed the subject to other topics, my mind was still busy processing how this whole boy girl thing worked.

So, from what I could gather, this courting game was partially about an attraction between the girl and the guy. But equally, or maybe even more important was the value of jewelry, even if she didn't like me so much. For the sake of a glimmering ring, I guess she would still be willing to endure a relationship with me.

It didn't really compute in my 5th grade logic, but you know these older guys had really been around. I was just a kid, and they were experienced 6th graders.

Mike and Punky were my consiglieres, my trusted advisers. So, I had to defer to their extensive knowledge of romantic protocol. As my pals drifted off to sleep, I was wide awake planning my first conquest. until the sun started to poke over the cascade foothills.

Within the week, I was city bound on the Greyhound bus to begin my pursuit of my girl.

Arriving in Seattle, I wouldn't have to travel too far to find that key that would unlock her heart. I knew right where to go. In the gift shop of the bus depot, they had an amazing assortment of rings, with colorful stones sparkling with hope under the florescent lights of the case.

How convenient. The bus station was the equivalent to going to Jared's for a ten-year-old, with a ten-dollar budget.

I gathered my courage, faced the sales clerk with the embarrassing task of buying her ring. I'd spent a couple paychecks from mowing our lawn on the gaudy, fake gold, pot metal ring with its bright red glass stone that was sure to dazzle her heart.

Stuffing the white cardboard gift box in my jeans pocket, I ran down Punky's script in my mind as the bus rambled down Interurban Avenue toward the Locke's Tukwila grocery store stop.

Picking out some candy for fuel for the long hill climb home, I debated whether I could or should go through with this and give her the precious gem.

I even thought about saving her a piece of my candy to up the ante, as I'd heard somewhere that girls like getting gifts of candy. But I ended up eating that idea as I climbed up the long, appetite building grade.

Flowers would have been far too melodramatic. Trudging up the hill, high on sugar from my Mountain Bar, I convinced myself that the prize of possibly winning her as my girlfriend was well worth the small risk of her rejecting me.

Sure, I hadn't had the confidence to really talk to her, but like Punky said, the irresistible allure of the ring ought to convince her of my worth.

Nearing home, I spotted my friends horsing around in the

Bergstom's yard, and I couldn't wait to tell them.

"Hey guys! Guess what? I DID it! I went and bought the ring" I announced with pride

"You WHAT?" Punky asked, with astonishment

"The ring. I got it. You know.... the RING.... Like we talked about..."

There was an awkward pause as I waited to receive my kudos and trophy from my buddies.

Punky laughed. Then he looked at Mike who while he wasn't quite as amused as the punk but did smile a little.

"You actually bought her a ring? What were you thinking? She's way out of your league! Ha ha!"

"But you said...."

"We were just kidding you big Dummy. Come on. Did you REALLY think she'd go out with you...?"

This time, the fat jolly kid wasn't laughing. But I figured he was probably right. Mike kind of looked at me with a sympathetic but agreeing gaze.

"How could you be so clueless?" his expression scolded.

Mike's reaction wasn't quite as callous and blunt as Punky's, but clearly, he didn't think I would have taken this game so far.

So ultimately, I did take Punky up on his ring toss idea. But instead of embarrassing myself any further with false hopes by trying to give the ring to this girl, I chucked the cheap ring into the browned grass of a Tukwila drain ditch, flinging away my dreams of making my first love be with a California Hottie.

And wishing that I hadn't wasted my time, or my high hopes.

While it didn't entirely destroy my hopes for a love life with an attractive girl forever, it definitely did set me back a few years. From that point on, I kept my impossible longing for this girl hidden behind my red blushing face. And kept the foolish notion that I once had, of being capable of pulling off this silly serenade, buried in my small vault of broken dreams.

That vault would slowly get bigger over the years, but for whatever disappointments we suffered, there was always something to get your mind off your troubles. Like going to the movies.

8

DRIVE INS AND MATINEES

We would have loved to sit on the couch in front of a 65-inch screen with a remote bringing up any one of thousands of movies at our command. But it wouldn't have been nearly as memorable as sitting in the back of your station wagon in your jammies watching a movie with your whole family on the 65-foot movie screen at the drive in was.

There were quite a few drive-in movies theaters in the 60s. You'd know them by their dazzling marques with chasing lights surrounding a reader board announcing this week's feature.

Drive ins were always concealed by groves of 75-foot-high Poplar trees, creating a natural curtain., They often had a small playground, so the kids could slide and swing while Mom and Dad gathered popcorn and candy from the snack bar before dusk brought the screen to life.

Tom and Jerry, the Pink Panther or the Road Runner were usually the opening acts. As the main attractions would begin, the children would start dozing off. Then Moms and Dads could then be able watch the movie in peace.

The darkness would also wave the starting flag for teenagers to begin their make out rituals in the moonlight. Snuggling in cars they borrowed from their parents for the night.

More than once, with their minds clouded with great expectations, these teens would start to drive off with the speaker still attached to the window as they left. And return home with no window attached to the door.

It would be quite a while before they would get to use the car again.

Locally, we had the Midway, the Duwamish and the El Rancho theaters to choose from. Once upon a time, High Schoolers would try to dodge the admission fees, by sneaking their cars in through the unguarded exits lanes.

But the theater owners got wise and installed spikes to pop your tires if you attempted to slip in through this back door.

It was just as bad of an offense to bring Dad's car back with two unrepeatable flats as it was to return it with a busted-out driver's window.

So, Plan B, was to load your trunk full of your friends and then sneak them out in the darkness, once safely inside.

The El Rancho rendered that scam obsolete by charging by the carload instead of per person. That pretty much put an end to the body in the trunk capers. It just wasn't worth it anymore.

Because if you were taking your girl out to the movies, it was a poor way to impress your her by throwing her in the trunk of your car. And if you were going with your buddies, you'd just all chip in for the carload price at the El Rancho.

The movies were always second run there, but in high school the Animal beer tasted just as good no matter what was showing on the screen.

But gradually, as cable TV expanded our 4 channels into hundreds, and home video gave us access to any movie anytime, one by one, the Drive-In theaters began to fold.

Midway Drive In converted to a huge Swap Meet, where people turn their unwanted belonging into a few bucks and others could find great bargains. If we had to lose it, it was cool that it became something nearly as cool as the theater itself was.

But like so many other treasures of our past, the swap meet metamorphosed into another huge home improvement center. Both Swap Meets and Drive Ins have now been relegated to the history books of our minds.

On weekends, winter or summer, rain or shine it was always the thing to do to go to the matinees up at our local theater, the Lewis and Clark.

Moms and Dads would drop us off before the movie, and be waiting for us after the show. Not only would we get to see a great movie, but you would all be on the same page with your school chums for talking about it on Monday during the school year.

There was nothing like a double Disney feature, and a big bag of popcorn with your friends to fill a Saturday afternoon.

I had a serious crush on Halley Mills, and I recall leering at her in "Moon Spinners" on the big screen. Miss Mills would be the queen of my dreams until Marsha Brady came along in the early 70s, dethroning Halley.

We would go so often, that the theater felt almost like a second living room. After the show, we sometimes stopped in at the adjacent Bowling alley for a few frames or a game of pinball.

I always paid admission. But not everyone did. When the lookouts established that there were no ushers were in the auditorium, some kids would sneak over to the exits, and quietly let their friends in.

They were sly, and I don't remember anyone ever getting busted for scamming their way in to the movie without a ticket. Maybe the theater just let it go, thinking it was just a harmless prank. But I was too scared to even think about attempting such a dubious crime. Either pay for admission or make the admission to Dad, that I had cheated the theater after I got caught.

A thousand kids might have snuck in before me and never got caught. But I knew if one ever did, it would be me. Luck of the Irish. I wasn't so afraid of the police interrogation or the jail time, I just didn't want to end up in the court of Cliff Sweeney. Better to take me to prison, for my own protection.

Although I never tested the waters, I'm sure my Dad's threats were far worse than his actually punishment would be. Him being kind of a scary guy, kept me out of trouble. His bark was worse than his bite. But I'll tell you, that man could BARK!

Movie popcorn was more than just buttered. It was marinated in butter. Your fingers and face would be shining and slick by the time you finished. It beat home popped popcorn hands down.

There were no microwave ovens in the 1960s, nor air poppers. One quick way to get popcorn at home was to make "Jiffy Pop" Although it wasn't as easy as microwave, it was hands on fun as kids would shake the jiffy pop pan on the burner of the stove and watch the foil swell up as the kernels burst. But fun of popping aside, it just couldn't match the flavor of Movie popcorn.

Plus, it was the only place where you could find Dots, Good and Plenty, and Bon Bon's. Only in the movies.

Today's choices for watching movies are far more plentiful, yet somehow far less special and memorable than waiting for your big day at the movies.

9

GO OUT AND PLAY

For the most part, life in Tukwila was living the American dream. Dads worked, Mom's kept the house and made meals. And the kids spent a great deal of their time doing whatever they wanted in a world interesting and safe enough for them to roam freely in.

Roles were well defined. Dads were destined to work. Moms duty was to keep house and manage the children. Boys wore jeans and collected dirt and bruises. Girls wore dresses and played with dolls. And kids in general just had a lot of fun.

.Every kid that I knew, would go from crawling, to walking, to running as soon as possible. That's because there were so many things to see and do. And to get you there, you couldn't wait to get your wheels.

From your first tricycle to your 2-wheeler with training wheels to your treasured "Sting Ray" type bike with banana seat and ape hanger handlebars, Tukwila kids were a cycle culture. In our minds, we were all born to be wild, sporting our foot driven "choppers"

We would race them, jump them over ramps, and take them over every bump and chuckhole in the crater strewn streets of our city (Tukwila was notorious for it's battered, torn up streets)

Surrounded by nature, rather than danger, we pedaled far from home without fear. One of my favorite "runs" was to bike all the way down West Valley Highway to Kent with Lon.

Once there, we would stop at the Arctic Circle, for a burger, a bag of greasy fries that would soak the bag with oil, and a shake from one of their 30 different flavors.

Surrounded by woods thick with old growth Maples, Pines, Firs and surprisingly few Hazelnuts, we left no leaf upturned as we blazed trails, chased rabbits and squirrels and pretended to be little Lewis and Clarks.

Every boy loved to watch things explode, crash and burn. It was in our DNA. We'd bash our toy cars together and fly our toy airplanes into the ground, deliberately. And if we got hold of a string of firecrackers, it was mayhem.

I think that's why toys were built so sturdy and robust. So we didn't wreck all our stuff all at one time. They were manufactured to withstand the rigors of demented children, hellbent on destruction.

There was a big cliff not far from home that was too steep to ride our bikes down, but it looked like a great place to recreate those spectacular crashes that we saw on TV. After tossing many rocks down and watching them ricochet off the boulders at the base of this cliff, Lon had a great idea.

"Hey Ed, why don't we push your bike off the cliff and watch it crash, like in the movies?"

I was torn as I considered if I should actually roll it off the edge or not. Hey, I loved that bike. It was my pride and joy, so I didn't really want to see it get all banged up.

But Lon was right. It would look so cool bouncing and spinning off the steep wall before finally resting in a smoke like cloud of dust. The only thing missing would be it bursting into flames and the subsequent explosion.

Reluctantly, I agreed to give her the old "heave ho" And we sent it barreling down several times. It was just as cool as we had imagined.

Each time we walked down to retrieve my bike, it looked no worse for the wear. Factory paint was tough. And the small bends on the chrome fenders can be easily bent back in shape.

But on its last launch, we gave her a little extra oomph, and watched it bounce off the rocks in the craziest collision yet.

Again, it seemed to have come out pretty well, until I tried to turn the handlebars. "Oh No!" I cried. "Lon, we broke the stupid fork!"

Even though I had bought the bike myself. I knew Dad would be mad about it. Back in the depression, they appreciated and took care of their belongings.

He was going to throw me off the cliff when he found out I threw my bike off the cliff, I feared. Lon and I conferred and decided it was best that he should never discover what had happened.

On the next block there was a kid named John Johnson, and his Dad had a welder. I doubted that his Dad even knew my Dad, and he seemed like a pretty decent guy who probably wouldn't squeal on me even if he did know Dad.

So for five dollars, I got him to re-weld my forks. I had escaped the wrath of my Dad. But I told Lon clearly that my bike would no longer be used as a prop for our crash scenes.

"Why don't we use your bike?" I questioned Lon, recalling my sunken shoes at Harrison's pond.

"Because I use it for my paper route" he defended. "I have to keep it in good shape"

Fair enough. It made good sense. That bike was my meal ticket for candy at Franks Fixit when I was destitute, thanks to Lon's generosity.

I no longer had my route, but I still intended to keep my bike for riding. So we agreed. No more crashing anybody's bikes on purpose anymore. No matter how cool it looks.

Sometimes we'd head out armed with our Daisy pump action BB guns and stalk our prey mercilessly. Although we may have fired with the pinpoint accuracy of military sharpshooters, we would always return home without any game for Mom to cook up.

They say BB guns can put an eye out, but our guns couldn't kill a fly at point blank range. We did send a couple sparrows home with little welts on their wings and gave a rabbit or two a pretty severe headache.

There was never a lasting truce as we played "war" carrying our toy Tommy Guns and ducking behind trees to catch our "enemy" friends by surprise, battling each other in mortal combat on the nice days.

On wet days, we would work out our strategies with green plastic army men about to meet their makers as a rubber band from across the room could mow down a whole battalion.

Harmless fun? Well, we were warned that those rubber bands too, could also take out an eye. Yet I never met any kid who had to wear an eye patch, unless we were playing pirates.

Of course, my fire loving friend Lon would love to take the little green army men out on dangerous maneuvers far beyond the toy box. Outside, they may face the horrors of the Bic Lighter flame thrower or be caught in a deep foxhole as General Shankel would toss a whole string of Black Cat firecrackers in the hole changing the infantry men into the flying airborne, on their last missions.

Even with our heavy arsenals, not a one of us grew up to be a serial killer. Yet all of us were packing weapons before we had even lost our baby teeth.

Cap guns gave us the authentic gunpowder smells of the shootout at the OK corral as would try to send our best friends off to boot hill while imitating our favorite cowboy heroes.

Once while we were playing Cowboys and Indians, Bobby Sukert started taking the game a bit too seriously. Realizing that there was nothing deadly was coming out of the barrel of his six shooter, Bobby decided that using the butt of the pistol to the scalp of an invading Indian might help him to win the west.

I was the little brave that he sent running all the way home crying and screaming with a trail of blood pouring out of my head.

The Cowboys and Indians alike followed me back to the wigwam where they watched my mother patch my wounds and then make tuna sandwiches for the whole wild western crew.

My older brother Tom carried a high-powered slingshot known as a "wrist rocket" that indeed was powerful enough to take down a good-sized rabbit.

One day he loaded it with a big metal marble, what we called a "Steely" and the projectile sailed probably a half a mile through Bergstrom's pasture and broke the Shankel's bathroom window as my friend Lon was relaxing in his bathtub.

While it was a random unintentional fluke, I'm sure the little green army men would have felt vindicated by this stroke of luck.

One of my favorite battles was when my Tom, Joe Bergstrom, probably Howard Harrison, and the other big kids joined forces with us to take down the Moores and Islers, whose properties bordered the Bergstrom's pasture.

I doubt there was any provocation from those quiet and peaceful neighbors. But Tom and Joe just wanted to demonstrate their prowess and flex their muscles. We little kids were indifferent to whatever political differences had spurred this conflict. We were just following orders. It was patriotism to our family that put us on the battleground.

Our big brothers plummeted them with bushels of apples, and pears from the Bergstrom's fruit trees, while we young kids lobbed sticks, and fern spears over across the Moore and Isler fences.

The Moore brothers fought valiantly, but in the end, it was clearly a victory for the Bergstrom/Sweeney regime. No major casualties, but their yard looked like a fruit salad garnished with garbage by the time they retreated.

And any carnage that had come from across enemy lines would soon be cleared by the hungry Sonny, Mary Bergstrom's Palomino horse.

Of course, Jeff Moore was still my friend after this war, and we would still be friends, all throughout my youth. But a serious message needed to be sent to the Moores and Islers that day. What the message was, I'll never know. But we delivered it in an unforgettable manner.

But life wasn't all picnics, pretend, sleepovers and war games. At the tender age of 5, the demands of the real world of education rudely crashed our never-ending party. Each year, as the days began to get a little shorter the perfection of summertime would be tainted by reminders of our pending doom.

"Back to School" sales fliers were stuffed into the Seattle Times. And Mom would take the whole tribe to the Wigwam store for new shirts, pants, tennis shoes and school supplies.

While I've been told that the girls got excited about their new wardrobes, my buddies and I would have been content with our torn knee wranglers, learning about life in the school of hard knocks in an endless summer rather than getting a real education.

We always dreaded returning to the grind that began on our first day of school and ended when we were handed our diplomas. But it was all part of the growing up package.

And today remembering how I thought I would have liked to be a school dodger, I scratch my head and ask, "What was I thinking?"

In reality, at 5 years old, the wheels of life were just starting to roll. And by dropping out, I would have missed out on a whole lot of fun.

10

SCHOOL

I had no idea what I was getting myself into. Although I had it pretty good at home, the thought of attending Kindergarten seemed like an adventure that I might savor for a little while. I mean the Moms all promoted it like they were Army Recruiters.

The military tells you that if you sign up you will see the world, expand your horizons, grow up to be a man and experience life. "Be all that you can be" They fail to mention about the tough rigors of boot camp. Or that while you're having such a great time seeing the world. the enemy will be shooting live rounds at you, aiming to kill.

Regarding starting school, the Mom's told you that they were so "proud of you" That you're "really growing up" That you're going to meet new friends. and learn new things every day. It sounded interesting. Something we might like to try for a couple weeks. But they didn't tell you that you'd be getting locked into the system for the next 13 years.

You just didn't realize until those schoolhouse doors closed behind you for the first time, that your gravy train has just made its last stop, at the Salt Mines.

In 1961, the outside walls of Showalter Elementary School were as pale as the faces of the children who were imprisoned inside. It was nicknamed the "Pink Prison" There were two wardens who ruled the institution with iron yardsticks.

Principal Wayne Weber was a short, stern man with a silver brush-like crew cut. He seemed fierce and menacing with his blazing eyes, that seemed to capture our every move. Nothing got past his eagle watch, and as the kids marched off to their classes, you'd hear his penetrating voice,

"Tuck your shirttails in", "Comb that hair", "No running in the halls"

I don't remember Mr. Weber ever administering any corporal punishment, but his admonishment of the troops never ceased. His reprimand was all it took. He was not a man to toy with. You didn't play with Mr. Weber.

In first grade, we had our first school portraits taken. Not only did I have big brown eyes on my photo, I also had also grown a big brown nose. I thought picture time might be a good time to "Suck Up" to our intimidating leader.

I knew the staff also had taken pictures, and while I had no intention of posting it on my wall, I figured asking him for a wallet sized picture of himself would flatter our commander in chief. And get me on his good side.

"Mr. Weber, CAN I have your picture? I begged, hopefully.

"MAY I have your picture, you are supposed to say!" Webster corrected me with a roar and a scowl, as he handed me one of his smiling glossies.

It's going to be a long year, I thought as I tried to decipher what my grammatical error had been. Hey, I was only a first grander. I didn't have a bachelor's degree in English.

Vice Principal Robert Ridder was a tall, lanky man with a cheery smile and a bow tie. He seemed to have a genuine interest in promoting the joys of learning, as well as a love for the kids in his flock

While he didn't scold or lecture much as Webster did, Ridder instead let his paddle that hung on his wall do his talking.

After one or two disciplinary sessions in Mr. Ridder's office, most of us would make sure that either we didn't do anything wrong ever again, or at least didn't get caught at it.

My first Teacher was Mrs. Houston. She looked to be a 100 years old if she were a day through five year old eyes.

A plump lady, dressed in long drab dresses of dark green and gray, Mrs. Houston sported the traditional schoolteacher bun hairstyle that had been fashionable since the 1860s when she was born.

With her hunched over posture, she terrified me immediately. The resemblance to the witch in Hansel and Gretel was horrifying. I scanned the room looking for a hot oven and sniffed for the odor of burning children. But when she smiled to the class and spoke, my racing heart receded, and I learned to relax in her presence.

Mrs. Houston wasn't at all as she appeared. She turned out to be a sweet, kindly woman who seemed to be there to only to facilitate the merriment here at this fun factory.

I don't recall learning much in Kindergarten, other than the alphabet and numbers. It was mostly coming up with craft projects like making imprints of our hands in clay for hanging on our Mom's kitchen walls. Displayed along with our brother's and sister's impressions from the same place, at a different time. Or making Christmas cards for our Moms and Dads.

Other than sending us home with such tokens to convince our parents their tax money was well spent, it was predominantly just play time all the time, just like at home. And getting to meet other little twerps like ourselves.

With the looming threat of being sent to see Weber or Ridder, there were very few behavioral problems. Because of that ever-present danger of being punished in the principal's office, we really watched our P's & Q's. as we learned how to write them.

Showalter was a old school with a lot of spooky sounds. The radiators would clang. The floors would creak in harmony with the rickety one-piece desks that should have been burned a decade ago.

And Mrs. Houston's bones would snap and creak too, adding surround sound to the creepy ambiance as she wandered about the classroom. And of course, there was the daily nap time.

The last thing that an excited five-year-old hyped up on sugar frosted flakes needed at midday was a nap. But every day at the peak of our fun. we would have to launch into our daily maneuvers of moving our desks aside and laying out our rugs for our faux sleep session.

I seem to recall Mrs. Houston used to read us a story first to tranquilize us as we laid on the shaggy mats, but it was never enough to lull us off to dreamland.

Afterward we would lay silently, eyes wide open, as the radiator and wall clock would tick off each of the 1800 long seconds of our half hour nap. Not one child slept a wink. But I do believe I did hear an occasional snore coming from Mrs. Houston's desk.

While faking sleep every afternoon got tiresome, our real song and dance would happen after nap time. In our toasty radiator heated classroom with 20 kids in various stages of potty training, along with a possibly incontinent old lady, adding livestock to the mix would have been sure to make our classroom become rather heady. But there actually was a stable of horses corralled in the corner of the room. Sort of.

Our dance props were cut down broomsticks with a plastic horse's head and reins attached to them. It was no Cavalia or Medieval Times, but Mrs. Houston taught us a catchy little musical routine that we would perform together as we rode our trusty steads.

The music was a variation of the old Laurel and Hardy theme. Can't recall the melody? Think of the old ditty, "The worms crawl in, the worms crawl out, the worms play pinochle on your snout..." and change it to "the Horse gets up" instead. That was our tune.

After a brief musical interlude, we would rise from our carpets choking our horses by their wooden necks, and sing together in discordant unison,

"The horse gets up, the horse gets up, the horse gets up in the morning...."

We'd run through that a couple times, and then really start trotting around in our little circles as the music droned on. Yee Haw!

School is to prepare us for living in the real world. And although I've never had occasion to use that particular skill in my work life yet, the song is still stuck in my head. Just in case I'm ever called upon to dance with a toy horse in some future nursing home agenda for our senile amusement.

I thought about dropping out of school after Kindergarten after I had experienced the freedom and leisure of my first summer vacation. But Mom and Dad wouldn't hear of it. So, in the fall, I found myself back at the gates of the Pink Prison for First Grade. One down, twelve to go.

I never thought of going to school as really being an academic pursuit. It was more of a social gathering as far as I was concerned. In as much as I could get away with it under the watchful eyes of teachers and the misters Riddler and Webster, I intended to have a good time since I was compelled to be there.

But Mrs. Jelma, my first-grade teacher, was determined to make education real. To her, the naps, crafts and lollygagging around on broomstick horses were kid's stuff. She was going to teach every reluctant little scholar to read, write and cipher before she released us onto the world.

We had little 6-year-old fingers, and Mrs. Jelma was teaching us how to write with these fat, oversized pencils on big one-inch lines.

I can understand the big lines for sloppy uncoordinated hands to practice penmanship with little developed finesse. But what was the purpose of those huge, tree log sized pencils that we wrote with? Maybe they figured they were harder to lose. Or to swallow.

But what about our MORALE? A little fun along the way to help us learn to love learning?

Frank Rineheart was sitting in the desk next to me, and I figured challenging him to a duel with our sharp writing utensils might enhance our learning experience. If I were teaching, I would encourage the children to be creative and enjoy the ride as they gathered their knowledge.

Frank seemed to agree that this was a fun, harmless game to learn both writing and self-defense. But as soon as Mrs. Jelma noticed, the game was over. And our smiles turned to tears as we were sent off to Mr. Ridder's office to explain what we were doing.

"That's a good way to get lead poisoning" Ridder lectured as he grasped his well weathered paddle.

Although I found it fascinating to discover there was a good way, to get lead poisoning, I felt awful nevertheless. I might have inadvertently killed Frank with lead poisoning, and he was a good guy. I owned up to having started the mischief, but Ridder gave us both a pencil sharp reminder of our misdeed on our behinds.

I learned my first lesson that day. Make sure you have your fun when the teacher steps out for a smoke in the teacher's lounge. Not while she's on active guard duty.

But the bigger lesson I didn't learn until years later. There is no lead in pencil leads. It's graphite, and there was really no threat of "lead poisoning" But it was hardly worth appealing our sentences on that minor technicality so long after the fact.

My friend Cameron Wakefield was well acquainted with the paddling ritual in Ridder's office.

Years later he told me that once when Mr. Ridder was marching him off to the office for some infraction, he managed to postpone his punishment for a brief potty stop in the bathroom.

As he returned Ridder proceeded with Cameron's paddling. He took it well. Perhaps a little too well, the Vice Principal noticed. And his behind seemed a little too large and lumpy for a grade schooler.

"Okay Cameron. Let's have it...." Ridder demanded, with his outstretched hand.

Cameron reached into his pants and surrendered up his toilet paper padding. And then felt the full impact of his punishment. And then some, to pay for his ruse.

While old, Showalter was a showcase of a well-run institution. The floor tiles although faded and scuffed where polished and buffed its blemishes had the same luster as its fair complexion.

Lockers smelled of a fresh coat of paint each year and lined the hallways like a barracks. It wasn't a friendly ambience, but it was impressive in a militaristic way.

The antique wood doors and frames had inches of shellac giving the grain a depth like ripples of currents in a dark brown sea. The spotless classroom windows were fitted with small square frames that resembled bars for students to gaze out and imagine a world of freedom outside. In the rare moments when teachers weren't insisting on all eyes front and center.

Outside, the grounds were groomed and the lawns trimmed to the precision length of a teacher's crewcut. Clover, both 3 and 4 leafed were quickly eradicated.

No luck for dandelions or moss either. Nothing but perfectly spaced blades of ryegrass in careful formation, that seemed to know not to step out of line. Trees and shrubs were nondescript and knew their places.

The grounds were sharp, but not in an inviting manner. More like a cemetery where children's rambunctious, spirit and joy were put to rest before entering the facility.

Mrs. Houston had been a kindly, understanding mother substitute for her kindergarteners. But we soon found out she was the exception. Stabling our play horses and rolling up our rugs, we were about to advance to life in the cold cruel world, in this school of hard knocks.

The male teachers and principals wore suits with neckties. Ridder often choose a bow tie. The female teachers were dressed in modest, no nonsense attire.

A day in the classroom was like making a courtroom appearance. Whether they sat or rose, kids were always felt as though they were on the stand at Showalter.. But justice was arbitrary. There was no jury to challenge the stern, penal code of the Pink Prison.

We were sentenced to learn, as we learned to write sentences. Behind horned rimmed or thick black framed glasses, the teachers focused on discipline, order and COMPULSORY education. We were compelled to learn.

I think it was in sometime in first or second grade when my class transferred to the newly built Tukwila Elementary School. Hallelujah!

There were no bars, but big picture windows instead looking out on the fresh landscaping and trees of the woods. The playground toys were yet untouched by children's hands. Not one drop of blood from a skinned knee had yet dampened the blacktop. Chalkboards were jet black, and the room colors were bright pastels. This place was nice!

Everyone, students and teachers alike felt much more relaxed at Tukwila. Larry Snowden was a calm, laid back man, who would rather read the newspaper in his office with his feet propped up than to patrol the halls looking to find evildoers and bring them to repentance.

Comparatively speaking, this place was a breeze. They even had covered "breezeways" that provided a small refuge from the pounding Seattle rains when walking between buildings.

If Showalter had been a prison, Tukwila was barely a minimum-security unit. The heat was off, and we could loosen up the collars of our striped suits a little, figuratively speaking. I pitied our friends who were still in the "joint".

School lunches got a bad rap in my opinion. I mean, if you' were expecting a gourmet French chef to serve you a blue-ribbon recipe on every compartment on your tray, then maybe you should have gone to private school. Cafeteria fares were hearty, good tasting balanced meals.

Yes, they threw some vegetables at you, but mostly "candy" vegetables like corn and peas. They didn't try to trick anyone with Brussel sprouts or eggplant. And the insult of vegetables was BALANCED out by decadent desserts like the jewel of the kitchen, FUDGE GEMS.

Kind of like a rich chocolaty, "no bake" Mountain Bar, they looked like a pile of turd, with raisins undigested, poking out around the circumference. But if you could look past their appearance, your taste buds would only see the beauty of this treat.

Nonetheless, many of my classmates thought they looked disgusting. So, it was easy to negotiate a donation to my quest to find double or triple the calories I needed for the day. Remember, I was the fat kid.

Christmas and Thanksgiving were revered every bit as much as Halloween, both in and out of school. These were all part of our culture in America, and there was no fuss made about the ethics of any of them.

The Christians didn't take the schools to task regarding satanic origins of Halloween, and atheists, agnostics or people of other faiths didn't balk at Christmas, Thanksgiving or Easter observances. I didn't have any sense of anyone being offended by the practice of time honored American traditions.

Whether your family had deep spiritual convictions or not, at school we would simply glean all the fun out of the holidays and leave the controversies in the mine.

A Christmas tree, decked out with colored paper chains that had been manufactured by the class didn't equate to making a spiritual conviction. Everybody knew that.

If there was a Jewish kid, no one would make him feel self-conscious about Hanukah. Making Thanksgiving horns of plenty and cutting out Turkeys didn't subscribe you to a sect of Puritans. You were just honoring the history of Plymouth Rock.

Schools didn't take a stance on religion or politics. They did however teach us to respect the offices, like the Presidency. While they encouraged discussion of the issues, both historical and of current events.

Instead of telling you what to think about an issue in social studies, they would instead call on you unexpectedly, asking "What do YOU think about......" Especially when they noticed you hadn't been paying attention.

While there were many men and women serving in the military across the country in in Vietnam, there were lots of kids in uniform in the classrooms.

Cub Scouts, Boy Scouts, Bluebirds, Brownies, Girl Scouts all proudly wearing their uniforms with neckerchiefs, sashes and awards pinned on them. They were welcomed in and by the schools without having to compromise or rewrite their agendas.

This represented freedom to people at the time. Kids were free to participate if they were aligned with the codes and statues of the organizations, or to not partake if they didn't. And they were free of course to start their own organization if they didn't feel they were a good fit.

That was America in the 60s, land of the free and home of the brave.

I have to admit I was a lazy student pretty much all the way through school. Report cards would always say things like "Eddy is bright, but he's not living up to his potential" Or "Eddy has the ability to perform well, but he doesn't finish his assignments".

So, I'd have to have the long talks with Dad regarding my grades, where I'd try to convince him I wasn't as brilliant as they thought I was. I did successfully snow them when it came to math. Mom had admitted she struggled with learning it, and I convinced both my parents that my inability to grasp higher mathematics was probably genetic.

You'd better knuckle down and get those grades up, or you'll end up digging ditches when you grow up". Dad warned.

While he meant well, in adulthood I discovered construction workers made some great money. Often more than their college graduate friends. They stayed in great shape and saved their parents thousands of dollars in tuition fees. My poor grades could have been a blessing to everyone. But being put on restriction until I improved my marks kept me from flunking out, for the greater good.

I ended up becoming a crane operator. I think I could have learned the ups, downs, backwards, forwards, lefts and rights in less than 13 years of school. Yet, the extra knowledge did come in handy at times.

Even adding the compass directions of North, South, East and West, I probably could have nailed it all by the 6th grade. But school was much more than learning job skills.

Most of the life skills were learned outside of the classroom. And looking back, I'm glad I stuck with it. I got to meet a lot of interesting people in the process.

11

THE CAST

The characters in our 60s Tukwila Elementary School might have had different names, but we looked like the same stereotypical cast that was found in almost any school across the country. I've looked at the class pictures from other friends, and I see uncanny resemblances to myself and my friends, in almost every school class photo.

Every class had a token fat boy. That was me! Also, in the lineup were an apple-polishing teacher's pet, a bad boy, and a good girl. An athletic standout, and a weird kid. Leaders and followers. Scholars and flunkies.

I'll bet I could pick all these kids out on your picture as easily as you could pick them out on mine. I've often thought that school photographers all use the same picture and just change the nameplate to save money.

You could tell who was who, not only by how they looked and the things they did, but also by what they ate for breakfast.

Our weird kid wasn't a scary or dangerous one. He was just happy go lucky boy who hardly ever stopped smiling. He did have a strange, trademark ritual. He imitated the action of windshield wipers with his hands.

He didn't just wipe the imaginary glass occasionally, for a laugh. Rain or shine, inside or out, day in and day out, he kept wiping. He seemed to enjoy the laughter from the other kids. We thought that he was just funnin' around at first. But he would continue to wipe away all day, even after the laughter had died down. It didn't bother him that the kids laughed about it, and his routine never failed to amuse himself either.

I'm not trying to poke fun at him, I have no idea what kind of tragic circumstances had caused him to do what he did. Of course, it was a never-ending source of material for the school smartalecks to heckle him for it. Fortunately, I don't recall anyone bullying him for his compulsion.

Anyway, the weird kid probably started most mornings with a heaping bowl of Fruit Loops. He might have been a little "Coo Coo" for Coco Puffs" too.

Then there were the bookworms, wearing spectacles. Their eyes had failed them early due to the constant exposure to the white pages and inks of textbooks. They were painfully bashful and would avert their eyes when the teacher asked for volunteers to answer class questions.

Undoubtedly, they knew the answers. But they were too introverted to address the class. Bookworms came in both genders. They lived anonymous lives and would never reveal the personalities that they harbored in the modest closets of their minds. They easily pulled the "A Plus" grades in all subjects.

Somehow, I felt they missed out on much of the fun of growing up.But in their futures, they probably excelled far beyond the fun loving kids achievements. And may have even designed this computer that I'm writing this book on.

They would dip their spoons into the bland, healthy, but tasteless cereals like Wheat Chex, Raisin Bran or Grape Nuts. Reading the nutritional labels as they ate.

Academically, next came those, apple polishing, tattle tale, Suck Ups. They were first to be waving their hands in the air, with ready answers, both right and wrong, to the teacher's questions.

They passed out papers and were the first to sign up for any brown nose duties the teacher would delegate. And tattling on the kids who stepped out of line.

They were extroverts, but the rest of the class wished that they weren't. They did solid "B" work in class but would often be awarded with an "A", for their extra effort.

I think every one of these kids found positions in Human Relations when they grew up. Kissing up to the management, while interrogating and tormenting the workers.

And they are probably well loved by their colleagues today, as they were by the kids back then.

They didn't eat cereal at all. But would have a half a grapefruit and Melba toast for breakfast.

Right below them came the popular kids. They were the intelligent, clever, good looking, and talented bunch. From this gene pool came the leaders, the jocks, the cheerleaders, the student council members and the poster kids for any school publicity.

They had the ability to achieve all "A" s themselves, but that wouldn't be cool. And might get them labeled among the nerds or the suck ups. So their report cards would be a mixture of "A" s to showcase their intelligence, and "B" s to show that they were still hip enough to not care. .

These kids grew up to become Airline stewardesses, company

CEOs, airline pilots and Game Show hosts.

Those boys liked Wheaties, the breakfast of champions or Malt O Meal, which the winners used to "warm up" with. The girls ate either "Special K" or "Total" because they were Special, and Totally Awesome!

Then there were the average Joes, and the plain Janes who weren't smart enough to be the bookworms, weren't sacrificial enough to be the suck ups, and weren't cool enough to be popular. They received more "C" s than "B"s and if they ever got "A"s , it was only because of typographical errors.

They were "wannabes" in popularity but found great contentment in their average community where they were all no more or less cool than the rest.

They mostly turned out pretty normal and well adjusted. Just down to earth plain folks, who lived average lives in the common jobs, that make the world go around.

They thought they were being served Malt O Meal like the popular kids were, but they actually ended up eating Cream of Wheat or Oatmeal. But they liked it just the same, and never complained.

The "D" and "F" group were as diverse as their breakfasts. Some just didn't have the intellectual chops to make it, try as they may. But generally, they were nice kids, in fact extremely humble. What was in their cereal bowls? That was "Life"

The low-grade club also included one or two antisocial troublemakers who would often take exception to what others did or said. It wasn't intelligence that held them back, but stubbornness and being too tough to be bothered learning all that sissy stuff. They loved to fight too.

They would eat "Sugar Smacks" for breakfast. And usually

ended up tearing cars apart at the wrecking yards. Or making license plates in the penitentiary.

Where did I fit into this sociological paradigm? I guess the lines were somewhat blurred for me.

If you asked my teachers, I was capable of pulling "A ", or at least "B" work. But I was too lazy. What did they know?

Being the fat kid, I wasn't quite cool enough to be in the popular kid's club, but they didn't really reject me either. They seemed to think I was good for a couple laughs now and then.

So, I kind of fell into that middle, average group. Because I was the fat kid, I was sort of a misfit too, so the low riders would let me in also. And I would even get extra lazy, scoring a "D" in history, just to give my membership in their group, authenticity. Besides, I hated history.

I never made much of a connection with the suck ups.

For my breakfast...I liked all the choices. Occasionally even a scoop of Purina Dog Chow from the Bergstroms. Hey, I was the fat kid, what did you expect?

But my favorites were the sweetest, most fattening, rot your teeth selections like Capn' Crunch, or better yet Quisp.

I think more important than learning history (which was my least favorite subject), school was about creating our own histories. And learning how to interact with a variety of people in life. Academic focus is pretty narrow in the real work world but learning how to get along with others was nearly as important as learning how to fight your battles.

12

FIGHTING WORDS

No grade school year would be complete, without George Howard and I having our annual donnybrook at the corner of the Tukwila school yard.

George and I were friends, and there was never any animosity towards each other, or any legitimate provocation for our scuffles. I think it was mostly out of tradition that we would grapple about once each year.

I think we started out with just some good-natured pushing and shoving, which soon escalated into hammerlocks and full nelsons.

In a fist fight, I would have emerged a bloody mess. But we would just wrestle around in the shadow of Altmayer's pasture, until one of us would be rendered helpless and forced to say "Uncle". And we would emerge as we came into our battles, as friends.

With muddy knees, maybe a tear or two in our clothes we would exit the school yard on 58th Avenue, stopping to rest and taking a ride on the Chance's tire swing. Sometimes I won, other times the crown went to George. By the time we passed the Bistlines, the Longs, and the Howats, any small wounds we may have suffered would have already healed.

"See ya tomorrow George" I'd say as I veered off to take the shortcut home through Tod and Darcy Pesika's yard.

"Okay Ed, see ya" George would respond with a wave.

That's how fighting was in Elementary school in Tukwila.

There was no hatred or need to seriously hurt each other. Just a couple boys blowing off steam, maybe clearing the slates. And testing their own prowess against one another.

In Junior High School, the confrontations became more serious, and the stakes became higher. These were more like prizefights. Fisticuffs would often break out in the hallways. To be watched by a thick crowd of cheering spectators spreading out from the ring around the boxers, all the way back to the steel lockers. All begging for blood.

Often the trophies they took home were black eyes, bloody noses and at times, a new-found respect. But these battles weren't cute little squabbles in the sod between little kids. These were brutal. bare knuckle batterings from high strung adolescents packing all they had into every punch.

I was kind of a late bloomer, and I managed to keep my childlike face clear of the swinging fists of these rapidly growing young men. If not, I would have ended up looking one of Rocky's hanging sides of beef that he used to practice on before facing Apollo Creed.

One particularly intense and gruesome fight took place in the Showalter Cafeteria between some feisty new kid and Shawn Wright. I don't remember what the beef was that day, or who it was that prevailed.

All I remember is one of this pair had grabbed the other in a headlock and charged with him like an angry bull, slamming his eye hard into the coin return handle of a vending machine somewhere between 5 and 10 miles per hour.

Oooh!

It caused a pretty gnarly injury, and I thought the kid was going to lose his eye.

It would take a pretty ugly matter for me to be willing to sacrifice body parts for. Either mine, or my opponents. Witnessing this brawl, made a compelling case for the value of using negotiations instead of eyeballs against vending machines.

There were a lot of venues around the Showalter, Foster vicinity where kids could hold a planned fight. But some of the most unholy beatings took place in the parking lot of the St Thomas Catholic church.

I'm not sure if it was because of the proximity to the school yard and its relative isolation, or because it would have been a convenient place to give the loser his last rites. But these fights seemed to draw more attendance to the church than the Masses on Sunday mornings did.

"Meet me after school in the Church parking lot" one would beckon.

The challenge would be accepted and overheard by a half dozen students on their way to class. News traveled fast, and each of those would whisper about the upcoming event to another half dozen in their next period class.

In the hallways at the next break, it would be the talk of the Campus.

"Going to the fight?" one would ask

"Wouldn't miss it" another would answer.

I'm not absolutely sure who Delbert Webster was taking on. But probably, it was Delbert against Paul Pearl at one of the most promoted and publicized bouts in school history.

It was our version of Mohammad Ali vs Joe Frasier.

It looked like everyone, but Howard Cosell was going to be at ringside.

As school dismissed, the adjacent St Thomas parking lot looked like Madison Square Garden, or Caesar's Palace. With huge throngs of students marching through the church gates, as the two fighters rolled up their sleeves for the anticipated fracas in this "Promised Land"

It was quick and bloody. And Delbert was gloating proudly after his victory.

Delbert was a friend, so I asked him, "What did you have against the guy?"

"Nothing" he revealed

Puzzled, I asked, "Well why did you want to fight him?"

"Because I just thought I could take him" Delbert answered.

Fair enough.

Our class in particular was noted for a different kind of fighting that would leave our clothes a mess, but without so much as a scratch on us.

Lots of people didn't care for the school lunches. Personally, I liked them, but that's just me. Anyway, it wasn't uncommon for students to toss their lunches before they had finished eating.

But it was common for students from the class of 74, to toss those leftovers in each other's faces, rather than in the waste cans.

These were wild, funny, and intense, food fights. Not being willing to part with my own lunch, I would sit and watch them amused, as my friends would share their food with each other in this most unorthodox way.

A kid would take a swig of their milk And I would watch it come squirting back out of his nose in a burst of laughter, as he would fling the open carton across the room spraying its contents across diners at several tables. Chocolate or regular, it was just as hilarious either way.

But after that, it was ON.

With the abandon and anarchy of an old west bar fight, all civility was lost. The only punches thrown were fruit punches. The staff "Sheriffs" could not contain the carnage. The kids would shoot up the place in a hail of fries and endless rounds of half eaten sandwiches.

Like fireworks, the ceiling was painted with foods of every color and description. When the pandemonium settled, the floors and tables were like one continuous chef's salad of meat and vegetables, with desserts as it's croutons.

So many were involved in the mischief that no one could be implicated. It happened all the time. It was a riot of fun for the kids. Not so much for the janitors and even less for Mr. Weber who equated it to a real riot in his Pink Prison.

In his "press release" the following morning on the school PA system Weber would denounce our entire class.

"You're all a bunch of AMIMALS" I clearly remember were his exact words. I think we took that as a compliment,

But we were loyal, faithful fun-loving animals, who would never betray our herds.

There were no vermin within our pack to "rat" on the others. Of all the lessons that I learned throughout school, the value of community and solidarity, in both our good deeds and our misdeeds has been one of the most valuable and enduring lessons to me.

13

TRICK OR TREAT

It was never about the costumes, or devil worship, or even about the Candy. The candy part was a sweet deal, make no mistake. But it was mostly about running with the pack. Like Jesse James gang, scoring the loot while sharing in the camaraderie with your buddies was what Halloween was all about..

Today's trick or treating is a highly supervised, chaperoned affair with the parents parading their little Spidermen and Princesses to only a handful of stores and their closest neighbors. Until their tiny buckets are only half full of bite sized treats.

Micromanaging the fun times too much, makes trick or treating an exercise rather than an experience. I guess we lived in safer, less threatening times. Mom and Dad stayed home to pass out treats to other bands of spooks who haunted Tukwila.

In the 60s we roamed the streets in little bands of friends on All Saints night. And at the end of the night, it was time to prove which of us had the biggest sacks.

Our Halloweens were intense scavenger hunts where we would scourer many blocks in search of the biggest bags of the biggest bars of candy. It was like a fishing derby.

Mom and Dad tagging along would have ruined our fun.

Halloween was our night to prowl, and to HOWL.

We would carefully chart our paths, crunching the demographic data from last year, to assure the highest yields from only the most affluent apartment houses.

Time was of the essence, so we couldn't be bothered with the far apart doors of houses with their long driveways. Racing between the closely spaced doors of highly populated apartment buildings was where the real money was at.

Some of the smart kids would hit the bricks armed with pillow sacks. But I recall always setting out with a big brown paper sack. After one or two soggy, ripped bags on a rainy Halloweens, I learned to double bag of my loot sacks, But I always left the linens on the bed at home. I wasn't THAT smart.

We were well versed in the economics of candy.The expected payout for our "Trick or Treat" recitals was either one Jumbo Butterfinger or a Baby Ruth, the king-sized bars.

If you were handing out Big Hunks, we'd have to grab two, because they were so thin. As were Hershey bars, whether plain or almond. If you were dealing in penny candy, you'd better shell out a good handful or two to keep from offending us little goblins.

We could smell a "health food" scam a mile away. Those were not treats. They were evil tricks by homicidal maniacs, intended to give little kids some very UN-Happy Halloweens.

Mom and Dad had warned us about taking anything homemade or unwrapped. Eating these might have blown the flames out of our little Jack O Lanterns, for good.

For example, those 'eat one a day, keep the Doctor away' apples, were sure to be loaded with razor blades. And guaranteed to send you to the emergency room, we'd always been told. And homemade popcorn balls were probably merely a Trojan Horse full of *strychnine. We* were instructed to smile, say "thank you" and throw them away as soon as possible.

And although there wasn't any toxic payload in those carrot or celery stick treats, it was just plain MEAN to give us something so wholesome after we'd come all this way to beat on your door. Come on. It's Halloween. Give us something to rot our teeth with!

Some houses would pass out nickels or maybe even dimes. Although we could purchase a Three Musketeers bar later with the coins, doing so wouldn't fluff our bags tonight. We needed bulk to help us weigh in heavy at the end of the night.

I'd heard about Halloween pranks like toilet papering trees and houses, egging cars, and soaping door handles. We didn't have time for such nonsense. For my friends and I, it was just about getting a little sugar. We always opted for sweetness over meanness on All Hallows' Eve.

And how sweet it was! We should have had enough Candy to last all winter, until the Easter Bunny replenished our sugar shelves. But instead we would eat ourselves sick for a couple weeks and be back to our Franks Fixit Shop runs before Thanksgiving.

It all balanced out somehow. My friends might have started out at 65 pounds, gathered 30 pounds of sweets that they would consume over the next, two weeks. They would burn off most of the calories and end up weighing 67 pounds but growing an inch and a half.

I might have started out at 80 pounds, collected 33 pounds of candy, and finished it in a week and a half. I would burn off 2/3s of that, and finish up weighing 90 pounds and growing two inches, in the waist. I never was very good at math.

But I repeat. There was never anything sinister about our escapades. And our costumes were never meant to either be cute or raise fear. It was just a masquerade to teach us the logistics of running a successful business operation. And give us a little kick start on our future cases of diabetes.

14

SECRET AGENT MOMS

I wasn't a bad kid, comparatively speaking. I knew kids that lived down by the old Central Elementary School who made my friends and I up on the hill look like saints. We were the kids in Scouts, who took piano lessons, and sat in the wooden pews dressed in bow ties trying to keep still on Sunday mornings.

But while we "goody two shoe" kids were doing someone a good turn daily, those Central kids were turning over their garbage cans. Or placing flaming bags of dog turds on porches, ringing doorbells and dashing off before the old man would burn his slack cuffs in a smelly stomp.

Every kid in those days learned early to cover their tracks to avoid prosecution for whatever crimes big and small they were committing.

But those Central kids were experts. If they had been convicted of all their many infractions, they probably would have spent their youths in the state penitentiary in Walla Walla rather than in the Pink Prison of Showalter.

Some of the minor trouble I got into was caused by my insatiable appetite. My parents were always trying to help me with my weight problem by preparing me diet foods and monitoring my access to the contraband foods. I realize they were really trying to do me a big favor, but I always lacked willpower when it came to little desserts with big flavor.

We had a big ceramic cookie jar, but it was kept up high on a shelf. Its lid alarmed loudly with its glass on glass sounds whenever it was lifted or replaced on the jar.

I became quite skilled at stepping softly, and silently moving a chair to the cabinet. Then muffling the lid with the padding of my fat fingers as I stuffed my pockets with toll house cookies.

But even with all my cunning and ability to crack the cookie safe unseen, on laundry day the crime lab would discover the cookie crumbs in the bottom of my pocket. And I would crack under Mom's interrogation.

I never had my rights read to me once. Indeed, in America children were innocent until proven guilty. But circumstantial evidence was more than sufficient to convict us in our own homes.

Back then, children would have never even considered suing their parents. And yet there were no disgruntled students shooting up the schools.

Fear factor wasn't a reality show on TV. It was the key to deciding to do what you're supposed to do, over what you really wanted to do.

In fact, for me and many others, the threat of consequences was enough to keep us on the straight and narrow. I would have had much more fun, but grown up far seedier if it hadn't been for the dread of punishment.

There was a growing trend for parents to subscribe to the anti-corporal punishment teachings of Dr. Benjamin Spock. a lenient child rearing guru. A distant relative of the Vulcan Mr. Spock, the

Doctor advised parents not to discipline, but to allow them to explore their own creativity and individualism by doing as they pleased. Let them find their own way he suggested. And many of those kids found their way to prison eventually.

Wisely, most of the parents and our schools around Tukwila abhorred Spock's theories. Opting for the tried and true, "You'll be sorry" approach to preventing misdeeds. Schools and parents worked in tandem to maintain order.

There was a well-defined criminal justice system for children that was despised by the kids. But was an effective deterrent to mischief.

For the most minor infractions, the teacher would send you out of the classroom and make you stand out in the hall. You were lucky to receive that sentence. Or staying after class to write "I will not..." do whatever you had done until the blackboard was full of your penances.

For a more severe misdemeanor, you might receive a swat or two, either in the hall or in front of the class to deter any other lawbreakers from repeating your sin. No kid was ever maimed by these minor thrashings, but they would think twice before re offending.

If your crime was sinister enough, you'd walk the green mile to Superior Court, in the Principal's office.

I think the principals stopped by the gym every morning to keep their paddling arms in top condition. You might shed a tear or two when the principal paddled you. But if he sent you home with a note detailing your dastardly deeds, then your weeping was just beginning.

"I got paddled at School today" would not arouse the sympathy of your parents. Neither would they call the media to publicize the injustice. Or even consult their attorneys to launch a class action suit against the school district. Instead you'd be looking at an even worse punishment, followed by a lengthy parole or restrictions and grounding.

Consequently, teachers were able to teach, and didn't fear their students. If they demanded order or quiet in the classroom, all hands would be folded on the desks. Every mouth pledged allegiance to the flag. And if you were chewing gum, you had better have brought enough for everyone.

Yet evidence of gum chewing could be found beneath every desktop. A rainbow of colors, flavors and bacteria from decades ago clung any loose boards securely to the framework.

Dads could be strict. They had a Judge Judy sensibility to the nonsense of children. Their baloney detectors were well calibrated, and extremely accurate. They understood the psyche of kid's naughtiness. Probably because they too had done the same things as kids themselves. But they sure didn't have shrewd investigative skills like the Moms.

I think 60's Moms were specially trained by the CIA, FBI and the NCIS. Their detective skills were legendary. Some may call it "women's intuition" but I'm sure it was much more than some mystical sixth sense that would eat through the best of alibis. And solve the most mysterious of crimes.

"How did you know?" I would ask. It wasn't ESP, or Ouija boards, or Psychic abilities. Apparently, it was some Parrot, Macaw, or Myna Bird that did the talking.

My mom claimed that it was her, "Little Bird" that told her. I would have used my brother's Wrist Rocket to kill that "big mouthed" bird without any remorse, if had he really been the stool pigeon. But "little bird" was merely the code name for her espionage team.

But I'm convinced that all the mothers had a secret coalition among themselves. With data bases and surveillance, that rivaled that of the Illuminati. There was very little that escaped the all-seeing eyes of the vast network of Mothers, and their informants.

Even without today's security cameras, GPS, and DNA testing, Moms could collar a perpetrator almost anywhere. Forget about "Big Brother" Our little Mothers were the threat that took the place of our own consciences when deciding if the rewards of our evils were worth the risks of getting busted doing our dirty deeds.

Yet with our mobility and our counterintelligence we were often able to conceal some of our crimes in the isolated heavily wooded greenbelts of Tukwila. They might not have kept us from every form of mischief, but they did keep us sharp. And expanded our sense of awareness to avoid some consequences.

But those mothers didn't make it easy

15

THE LIBRARY

Decades before we had Google to provide instant answers to our every question or curiosity, every kid had to use his inner "Sherlock Holmes" to find his information.

Of course, our Moms and Dads supposedly knew everything. But for our betterment, they would force us to learn how to find those answers ourselves.

For a simple word, you might first ask Dad. "How do you spell Minnesota" for instance.

"Go ask your Mother" was his standard reply.

Of course, he would claim that he knew the spelling, but this wasn't his department. His mind was too full of work and Dad stuff .to be bothered with a kid's trivial spelling problems.

"Go look it up in the dictionary" Mom would suggest.

"But Mom, you KNOW how to spell it" I would protest

"Yes, I do. But you'll remember it better if you look it up"

She probably did know the spelling, but I think she had some kind of royalty agreement with the Webster's, and Funk and Wagnalls.

It was true in a way. If I had to dig out the dictionary, then take a wild guess at the spelling, that might be close to what I was looking for... then put the big fat dictionary away.... I'd REMEMBER not to ask questions the next time, and just try to spell it phonetically.

The minor markdown I'd get on my school paper for a misspelling, was well worth sparing myself all that trouble.

For the more complex questions, a kid had various sources. First you might ask your friends. The best they could offer you, were unqualified opinions. You would soon find out that they didn't know any more than you did.

For example, "Where do babies come from?"

The best information I could get from my pals was the Dads somehow initiated the process in some top-secret way, that only married people knew about. It was swearing to even say the name they called it. Months later, the Moms delivered them in much the same manner as we go to the bathroom.

Double checking with your older brother, he would laugh at your ignorance as though he knew the real answer. And thought that your theory was stupid. Whether he actually knew the answer or not was unclear. But he'd blow you off with a, "You're too young to understand.... Get out of here you little Turd"

It might be years before the truth would finally unfold, hopefully before you had found yourself a real girlfriend.

But the whole purpose of our existence according to our parents and teachers, was to gather the knowledge that we would continue to use throughout our lives. And without the all-knowing internet to provide us with an ongoing source of reliable information, we had to mine our textbooks and libraries for our knowledge.

There were a couple of handy tools that would have given our overworked minds a breather. But naturally, they were taboo. Learning was never meant to be easy. I guess they figured you would remember better, if you had to fight for your facts.

It would be many years before electronic calculators would be available. But some of us had those forbidden, "mechanical calculators"

These would let us add or subtract numbers by moving digits around with a stylus. But if you needed to divide, or God forbid ever needed to find a square root, it was either rack your brain, or just take your "F", and move on. I sometimes chose the path of least resistance.

Also, there were those little assignment folders called "Pee Chee's, They had a contraband multiplication table printed right on its flaps. Teachers despised both of these tools. They wanted us to be smart, and figure out how to add, subtract and multiply on our own.

But what could be smarter than using these resources to get answers twice as fast, with 100% accuracy? It seemed like the smartest way to roll to me. And more "Gentle on our Minds".

In the library, there were no computers to lead us directly to the answers we needed. But there were librarians whose appearance suggested their genus had evolved from owls.

Their attire was more prudish than modest, and their demeanor was 1 that of morticians devoted to maintaining the stillness and dignity of this learning mausoleum.

These mentors for tomorrow's nerds, hushed even soft conversation with piercing, "Shhhhhs", which were more disruptive than our soft conversation would have been to those serious scholars needing the quiet. But the librarians would be there to help you find your information, albeit in barely audible whispers.

I'm sure there must have been easier ways to file and categorize books, perhaps strictly alphabetically, but some visionary named Dewey had imposed his decimal system to challenge children to have to work for their brain food.

Then you had to look through a "card catalog" to find the number where you would find the book on the shelves. I'd rather be looking through the Sears catalog to find my next Christmas present.

But the library wasn't all bad. Encyclopedias were a quick way to find an overview on almost any subject. A book of limericks titled "Rocket in my Pocket" inspired me to start writing my own little funny rhymes and stories.

As a lazy student who figured that I might someday miraculously become a doctor, I loved to look at the human anatomy books. But I hated History.

I might not have known when Magellan circumnavigated the earth, but I did know where his duodenum was located as he did so.

And like most of the other little boys who were bored with everything else in the library, I always liked to check out the latest version of "National Geographic"

Before you draw the ridiculous conclusion that my buddies and I were interested in native cultures or geography, I must clarify that the appeal of National Geographic was not scholarly. Instead, It was the "Playboy" magazine for the under 12 crowd.

National Geographic would send photographers out to the distant corners of the world where the women had not yet discovered clothing.

While we might have been clueless about where the babies came from, we were well versed on where they got their nutrition from in the jungles of the Amazon or Africa.

We also spent a lot of time on the bra and pantie pages of the Sears and Penney's catalogs.

Occasionally, you'd have a buddy who found his Dad's stash of the real thing, an actual Playboy. We would end up gawking and laughing at the luscious, shapely women in the foldouts.

We didn't know why we did, but we knew we liked them, And were mesmerized by their seductive poses. It was kind of ironic, because at the same time it was kind of square to "like" girls, in the early years of grade school.

Dirty jokes (even if you didn't really understand them) and lewd comments were perfectly kosher and encouraged by the guys. But talk of "love" or even infatuation was an open invitation to ridicule.

So, 60's boys learned early from the Donald Trump book of "Locker Room Talk", And saying nasty things that you neither meant, nor understood about girls would earn you a great deal of clout around the clubhouse.

If you admitted to liking girls in general, or any particular one specifically, your chums would browbeat you relentlessly. In our twisted young definition of what was "cool", hanging with your buddies was "were it was at", and it was critical to maintain your macho image.

So, in this deceptive little game, we in the "Cub Scout set" kept their secret attractions toward girls to ourselves.

We had no knowledge of Venereal disease, but there was thought to be a serious risk of catching "Cooties" from getting too close to our female colleagues.

They were okay to look at, but you wanted to keep them an arm's length away to avoid the stigmas and teasing of your companions.

Having said that, I personally pretty much always had some girl pinned up on the covert walls of my mind. Early on, you wouldn't dare admit it to your friends. But as we approached the first double digit of 10 years old, an interest in the fairer sex was added to the list of acceptable "cool" things to discuss.

16

RAINY DAYS

It rains in the Seattle area. Not a just a little, but a lot. Slugs outnumber lizards 5 to 1 in and around Tukwila. Mold and algae thrive. So, there were many days between September and June when our Stingrays were garaged, and we had to find some indoor fun for ourselves.

We didn't have robots or computers. Our games were played on boards, not cellphones. But we didn't feel deprived. There were lots of ways to pass the hours away when the skies turned gray.

There were exciting new toys coming out every day. If you didn't have a particular one, then one of your friends probably did. In addition to my Tonka trucks, my favorite toys were really tools that would actually let you make your own toys. Such as the "Thingmaker" and the "Vacuform"

These were both machines that formed toys with molten plastic.

We molded "Creepy Crawlers" out of a syrupy, toxic smelling potion called "Goop". We would bake these durable rubbery snakes and spiders to scare people with (especially the girls) in the Thingmaker.

The molds were quite realistic, and the Mattel toy company had an obsession for the loathsome and macabre. They really knew how to pack the "Creepy" into our crawlers.

The Vacuform used an electric burner to melt a small sheet of plate plastic on a metal frame until it reached the consistency of melted cheese.

Then we would flip this molten plastic over a mold with little suction holes. Pumping a handle made a vacuum that would pull the plastic tightly over our mold to create a perfect skin of the surface of whatever we were trying to duplicate.

Once you carved off the excess plastic, you had a flawless reproduction of your original. Although you only had about a 4 X 8 inch surface to work in, it worked very well.

I used to make some little plastic glider airplanes that would outperform the most of the flimsy store-bought balsa wood planes. But the technology would let you form replicas of almost anything you could fit onto the suction table.

For indoor fun, we also used to assemble plastic models of the latest year's cars. They were quite authentic looking, and great training for real life, as they would train us to breathe noxious glues and paints. Much like the carcinogens we would encounter in the factories we might eventually work in.

In addition to those two high heat appliance toys, product safety took a lower priority than making toys a fun to play with. before you became scalded or maimed.

Our toy guns were made of steel, and most of our toys had lots of pinch points ready to mangle our clumsy digits. Even the girl's Easy Bake Ovens produced temperatures capable of baking cookies or inflicting third degree burns.

But really our burns, cuts and scrapes toughened us up for life in the cold cruel world of work. The only thing missing was L and I for compensation for our missed play time due to injuries.

Legos were just introduced when I was a boy.   But there was plenty of construction toys.   Erector sets used real screws, washers and nuts to fasten metal beams together.

And there were wooden Tinkertoys using dowels that would connect using wooden hubs with holes drilled in them. I understand they are still available, but with plastic parts instead of wood.

We would build little cabins with Lincoln Logs.   Some of these were later destroyed by arson fires, explosions and swept away by flash floods from a well-aimed garden hose.

But my buddy Lon took the most interest in my chemistry set. We knew nothing of the science behind chemical reactions, but Lon would compound random chemicals together until we did get a reaction.   Sometimes it would bubble.   Other times it would heat up, or even smoke.

But the BIGGEST reaction we got was that of Dad busting open the door and saying, "What's that nasty smell?   What are you guys doing in there?"

"Nothing"

The chemicals bubbled furiously in the test tubes,

"Well, knock it off and go out and play"

A small green cloud precipitated in a flask.

"But it's raining...."

"So then put on your coats and go out and play...."

But when the weather cleared, my pyromaniac friend Lon talked me into trying an experiment using lye from Drano and Aluminum foil in a glass pop bottle.

The article in my "Little Scientist Encyclopedia" showed us how to make hydrogen. You would put some water, Drano and foil in the coke bottle and put a latex balloon on the lip of the bottle.

In a few minutes the balloon would inflate with hydrogen and the text suggested you could tie it off and it would float just like a helium balloon. I was about to let it fly away, when Lon said, "No... wait!"

"What for..." I asked

"Hydrogen is flammable"

"So?"

"So, let's blow it up" Lon said with a gleam in his eye.

Lon raced into the house and returned with a big wad of toilet - paper. We wrapped it around the balloon to use as a fuse. Lighting the long tail from the Charmin, we would step back and cover our ears and a few second later we got our first taste of "Fireball"

We called them our "Hydrogen Bombs" Although it was no Hiroshima reaction, we did have a blast lighting up our faces with little explosions.

When firecrackers were in season, we'd take two tin cans, and fill one partially with water. The other one would get a firecracker sized hole punched in the bottom.

We'd put a firecracker tightly in the hole and place it in the water filled can. The water acted like a seal to use the explosive force of the firecracker to launch the can out in the world's least aerodynamic rocket.

And yes, in the last century we had TV too.

Once upon a time, a fireplace or a piano was the centerpiece of a living room. But with the arrival of radio and phonographs in the early part of the twentieth century, such had become merely accessories to these new focal points.

By the late 50s and early 60's TV sets had become the king of the front room. They were often enclosed in beautifully stained and polished wooden cabinets. They sometimes also housed radios and phonographs too.

Our big screens were 25 inches, but a more typical size was the 19 inch portable TV. on a nice table surrounded by couches and easy chairs. Usually, the Dads would have the most comfortable lounge.

We didn't have 250 channels, big screens, surround sound, or 25 million colors in high resolution. We had 4 channels, up until 2 am. After that, only test screen images of an Indian Chief and the sound of his howling for the next 4 hours. There were 4 colors. Black, white, gray and, snow.

To change the station or volume, you had to get up and travel to the set. The closest thing there was to a remote control, was your Dad telling you to go change the station.

Depending upon which way the wind would blow, we might lose the picture all together. Although it was dangerous business on a slimy, mossy roof in the driving Seattle rain, Dad would risk his life to go up and adjust the antenna. As the NBC peacock would spread its feathers again, that was the reward for Dad's daring bravery.

As families, we cried together in the glow of the screen as we watched President Kennedy get gunned down in Dallas. We cheered together as we witnessed Neil Armstrong take his first incredible steps on the moon.

Unlike today, where we can get practically any program we want at any time, waiting for programs such as the annual broadcasts of "The Wizard of Oz" made them a real events.

"Waiting makes the heart grow fonder" may be a trite, old fashioned saying. But we discovered it was true in so many ways in the 1960s.

The scripts and the performances on situation comedies such as "I love Lucy" and "The Dick Van Dyke Show" were classically hilarious. The characters were believable, and for a half an hour we would be right there with them. Just as though we were part of their extended families. We felt we really knew the Ricardos and the Petries.

Walter Cronkite and Huntley / Brinkley delivered our news with sincerity. and journalistic integrity. We trusted them.

And the dramas and westerns would bring stories from faraway times and places into our own homes in Tukwila.

The whole world, and its highlights through the centuries were funneled through our antennas. And taught us there was life outside of the Land of the Hazelnuts.

It's no wonder TV was free back then. It paid its own bills through advertising. TV ads put many into the driver's seat at Hertz. And had us flying the friendly skies with United.

Television made you glad you used Dial soap, and really wishing that everybody else did too.

"With a rap of a hammer, and just a little bit more", we knew that Washington Builders would make that "Old place look like it never did before"

And we all knew what kind of kid ate hot dogs, Armor Hot Dogs. Fat kids, skinny kids', kids who climb on rocks. Even kids with Chicken pox.... Loved Armor Hot Dogs.

Sandwiched between your favorite shows, commercials couldn't be fast forwarded through.   But you really didn't want to miss them anyway.   Countless boxes of cereal were sold by them persuading kids to coax their parents into buying their specially marked packages for the sake of the cheap toy inside.

Without television ads, who knows? Your Dad might NOT have taken the family to, "See the USA" in his Chevrolet. Maybe TV helped you go on vacation.

And we all would have been cursed to life with "Ring around the Collar" had TV not suggested that our Mom's used Wisk.   Like polio, that insidious fabric killer disease had been eradicated, thanks to Television.

And who wasn't curious to buy a bottle of "Hai Karate". to see if you would really have to fight off the girls with martial arts, after splashing some on?

There were some harsh realities going on in the world, and television offered us a safe retreat from the brutality of the real world.

While a war was raging in the jungles of Vietnam, Gomer Pyle and Sargent Carter showed us life in the Marines could be funny too.

And when life really got tough, what better way to get away from it all, than to be cast away to a deserted desert island with Gilligan, the Skipper too, The millionaire and his wife.   The professor, Mary Ann, and Ginger"

While our parents struggled to make ends meet and keep up with the Jones, we'd both laugh at. and envy lucky guys like Tony Nelson and Darren Steven's on "I Dream of Jeanie" and "Bewitched'.

All it would take is a cute wiggle of Samantha's nose or a nod and a bow from Jeanie, to bring you whatever your needy heart desired.

Personally, I thought those guys blew it. Why, if I were Darren or Tony I'd have.... (Fill in the blank with whatever your heart desires)

TV was a social event. You didn't know how many friends you really had until you became the first family on your block to get your own Color TV.

Sports coverage became superb with the addition of cameras shooting the action from every angle. Programs like "The Wide World of Sports" and college and pro football turned potato chip companies into blue chip stocks. And created a steady stream of beer from the land of sky blue waters into our father's bellies.

But before Dad's games started in the afternoon, every Saturday morning was a marathon of cartoon heaven for us kids.

Johnny Quest, Tom and Jerry, The Bugs Bunny Road Runner hour for the kids. Our cartoon friends would keep us riveted to the screen for hours. And give Mom and Dad a little peace to be adults, as the kids would be kids.

For kids, the Seattle area was an entertainment haven. Some communities had their local childcare's television hosts and clowns, but none like the ones that we had.

Stan Boreson, Captain Puget, Brakeman Bill and especially J.P. Patches made the national stars like Captain Kangaroo, Buffalo Bob, and Bozo look like just a bunch of clowns.

Our TV guys had legions of little groupies, like the Patches Pals who would convince their moms to buy Sunny Jim Peanut Butter, Hostess Twinkies and Wonder Bread by the boatloads.

Seattle kids will carry our images of J P and Gertrude to their graves. J P was not only the mayor of the city dump, but he was the kingpin of kids programming.

His I.C.U. 2 TV actually seemed to allow him to look inside our homes and let us know where to look for our birthday presents. Yet it never seemed creepy.

His talking grandfather clock was a marvel of Claymation, puppetry or whatever sorcerer's magic made it come to life.

JP would pull cartoons right out of his cartoon hat. He was like a magician. And just watching him wake up in the city dump to his Spike Jones theme song each morning was worth us getting out of bed for.

JP Patches alter ego, Chris Wedes was really too good to be just a local entertainer. He should have been shared with the rest of the country. But we were so lucky to have him and Bob Newman (who played practically all J Ps sidekicks) here in Seattle.

Stan Boreson, Captain Puget and Brakeman Bill could have each been tops in their market in another town. But under the shadow of the Patches cast, all of them were tied for second place. There are no suitable replacements for any of these splendid actors for children today in my opinion.

As good as it was, TV was really just a side dish in the amazing feast of life for children in the 1960s. We watched it and enjoyed the heck out of it. But didn't live in front of our screens. There was far too much happening out there to spend our lives in here.

Especially on those rare occasions when Seattle's rain turned to snow.

17

A SLIPPERY SLOPE

It sounded just like the Seattle Seahawks had won the Super Bowl. Crazy cheers were heard from the kids in every house on every block when we would hear the TV announce early on a snowy morning:

"South Central School District 406, No School today"

Sometimes we weren't so lucky. As the first flakes began to fall, children would be praying for a real blizzard rather than just a dusting of snow. In order to avoid hearing that dreaded announcement that school would only be "running an hour late"

Understandably, our Dads, who had to drive to work on the slow and slippery roads hated it. But there were few things more exciting to a kid, than a school stopping snowstorm. One man's misery is another kid's pleasure.

Being in Tukwila on a snow day was like living in the Swiss Alps. The hills were alive, with the sound of laughter and metal blades of sleds slicing through the fresh snow.

Gott's Hill, Mountain Goat, Bremmer's were steep enough to accelerate our sleds up to nearly freeway speed. The many Hazelnut and maples were flocked like Christmas trees. And indeed, a snow day was the next best thing to Christmas for us.

Suiting up in multiple pants and shirts, two or three pair of socks, stocking caps, mittens, heavy boots, and big coats, we looked like walking piles of laundry as we stepped out into the chilly air. It was constraining, and it limited our flexibly. But those extra clothes not only gave us warmth but also padding for our inevitable falls and crashes.

We appreciated the warmness of our thick clothes as we whizzed down the hills, but it seemed like overkill when we sweated, climbing back up the little mountains for the next run, with our sleds in tow.

I cut my teeth in sledding in Altmayer's pasture overlooking the Tukwila Elementary school grounds. It had a pretty good grade, and a few bumps that added to the excitement. The only problem was the barbed wire fence at the bottom of the slope.

If you couldn't pull off your turn in time, you might get a little mangled up in the sharp barbs. But then again, you had several layers of cloth before the rusty metal of the wire would gouge your skin. But once we got a little older, we'd graduate to the famous big hills of Tukwila.

Mountain Goat, on the back side of 56th was long, and treacherous. The acceleration and exhilaration would just build and build as the run became steeper and steeper.

Then you'd hit that turn. While it wasn't that tight of a corner, you were going well in excess of the speed limit by the time you rounded that curve. And there were always cars to run into parked along the shoulders. I recall Mike Hanlon taking a pretty nasty header into the chassis of a station wagon. And leaving a little of his blood to stain the ivory white snow.

In another city, a hill like Gott's Hill would have been the bomb. But here in Tukwila, it was just a warm up in route to our version of

Mt Everest, Bremmer's Hill.

As first graders we would climb that hill daily to in our commutes to another work day at Showalter at the crest of Bremmer's.

So, it felt good to ascend to the peak, smile and give the school a good raspberry (or the "bird" if you dared). Then turn right around and race down the hill at dizzying speed.

Kids from all over the district, from every grade school to Foster High gathered at Bremmers.

There would be bonfires at the base of the hill. High School kids would be cupping cans of beer, while on lookout for the "Tuk Chucks", our local police. And the young kids would be sipping coco from steaming glass thermos.

There was always a heavy traffic of sledders zipping down the well packed ice at breakneck speeds. With cold wind whistling in their ears. Descending Bremmers Hill was like riding on the first big drop of a giant roller coaster. The most courageous of us would take a running leap onto their sleds for extra propulsion.

Some kids were too chicken for this intimidating hill and would just hang out and watch. Those who were brave enough didn't want to be caught "dragging their feet", because that would make you look like a "sissy".

But I admit that I did covertly dig my toes in on my descent to slow down a wee bit. It was just too crazy fast of a hill for me.

Snowball fights would frequently break out. Both fights for fun and for brutality.

Sometimes the older kids would show their superiority by plummeting the little kids to tears with a intense volley of fast pitched balls of snow.

Now and then, you'd discover those seemingly soft snowballs would have a rock core.

The worst way to get hit by a snowball was the side shot to the head. The force would bury the snow in your ear, packing it inside your eardrum painfully. You had to pick the pressed in snow out, bit by bit from your frostbitten inner ear.

It only took a couple of ear shots before you learned to keep your stocking cap pulled down securely over your ears.

Obviously, the sledding was much more fun than the snowball fights for the little kids.

After hours of climbing hills, wiping out in slushy pools and many snowball assaults, it was time to walk home shivering, in your soaked through clothes. We often returned with one mitten, your thermos either broken or lost. And we would be exhausted. Totally spent from the day's pandemonium.

Sleeping soundly that night with dreams of doing it again tomorrow God willing, if school was canceled again. Rarely would we be so lucky.

But whether or not we got a snowfall, there was always snow in the mountains each winter. And Ski Club.

"You want to go SKIING? Hey, if you want a broken leg, I'll BREAK it for you!

My Dad didn't mean it. He just had a very IRISH, interesting way of expressing himself. I think he'd had a bad experience on skis, and motorcycles once upon a time and wanted to spare his kids the misery he'd suffered. He tried to discourage us from both skiing and motorcycles.

But eventually he relented on the skiing, and soon I was standing at the bunny tow at Snoqualmie Pass about to learn how to ski. As with other sports, I was never a serious contender for the Olympics. I doubt I could have even been in the Special Olympics when it came to skiing.

Usually kids will progress from the "Snow Plow" to the "Stem Christie" to "Parallel", in their first season.It took me several years of intense practice and study. I guess I just wasn't a "natural", when it came to skiing.

Ours was only one of hundreds of yellow school buses pumping out black clouds of diesel soot on the pure white snow in the parking lot. All the kids were excited about zipping down the slopes with their brand-new K2 and Head and Hart skis bundled up in wool caps and heavy jackets.

But it didn't take long for me to start making scratches on the tops of their skis, as I would accidentally ski over top of theirs with my own before falling down flat on my face. Repeatedly.

After class, as the other kids were wearing out their gloves grabbing the rope tow, I was shivering over a steaming cup of Coco in the ski lodge trying to warm myself and ease my sore joints from my many falls.

The next Saturday, Dad would burst in to my room at the crack of dawn and flip on the light. I think he had been a Drill Sargent in a previous life.

"Get up" Dad would order

"Why?" I asked, deliriously

"It's time to go skiing...."

"But I don't want to..." I yawned.

"Look... I paid for it. You're going"

Soon I was back on the hill, in goggles, skis and poles.

I struggled to learn even the basics, I had to push myself to spend more time on the snow and less time sitting in the lodge.

I'd meet a lot of school friends on the slopes, as I would "bump", or crash into them while trying desperately to regain control of my skis.

Triple Olympic gold medal ski racer John Claude Killy was a renowned skiing hero in those days.   I think it was classmate Don Bohn who selected MY new nickname: "John CLOD Sweeney"

Unfortunately, it was not only fitting, but I became quite well known by that alter ego.

As bad as I was on skis, I did enjoy it, somewhat. After a (fairly long) period of time, I did learn to "V" my skis and keep my weight forward, so that I could actually turn, and traverse across the hill.

Everyone else was doing the "Stem Christie".   Some had even learned to do parallel turns.   But I was stuck in the dorky snowplow position, forever. I'm surprised they didn't offer me a job, to help clear the snow.

I recall the first time I was challenged to go up on the chairlift. "Big Bill" was the name of the chair.   The steepness of the run looked so daunting to me, as we rose up the side of the mountain.

"I don't know, I don't think I'm ready for this" I kept muttering to myself as our chairs swung in the snow flurries on the long ride up.

But as we reached the top and the "off ramp" and I stood up to push off from the chair, I saw the impossible steepness of the ramp.

"Oh no! I'm NOT ready for this", I shook.

Through my eyes, the ski jump looked like the ramp from Wide World of Sports that launched ski jumpers thousands of feet through the air before they tumbled disastrously in the snow, in the agony of defeat.

So, I panicked. Once my skis landed, I quickly shuffled around backwards and grabbed my chair as it was headed to the turnaround. Flabbergasted, the operator hit the stop button on the chairlift.

"What are you DOING?" He yelled though an ugly look on his face.

"It's too steep...I can't make it..." I responded, with my skis kicking a few feet above the ground.

"So... What are you going to do?"

I shrugged my shoulders, the best that anyone could shrug while hanging onto a chairlift, supporting themselves, wearing heavy ski boots and skis.

"Well, you need to let go.... Jump!" he told me.

As I hesitated, a chant began to grow from the impatient skiers in their stopped chairs, waiting to get off.

"Jump! JUMP!... Come on you IDIOT...JUMP!" they insisted, shaking their ski poles at me, like spears.

My arms were getting tired and getting yelled at was getting old too.

So, I let myself drop. After collapsing in the snow, I brushed myself off and snowplowed down the ramp.

I think there were patronizing cheers as the operator restarted the lift. Through a long series of traverses and a little side slipping, John Clod eventually made it back to the Lodge for a DOUBLE

Coco this time.

Billy Springer (Probably not related to Jerry Springer) was a kid also riding up on the ski bus. He wasn't all that much better of a skier than I was, but he always seemed to be having a good time. Seeing him smiling contently in his seat, I noticed he was holding a leather wine-skin in his hands.

"What do you have in there?" I asked. He handed it to me. "Take a shot"

He laughed. when I choked a little swallowing on the mystery drink.

"What is it?"

"Vodka, and Orange juice. A Screwdriver"

Mostly vodka. It only had a little orange aftertaste.

"Thanks" I said, handing the wineskin back to him.

"Have some more" he offered.

From then on, I always tried to sit next to Springer on the ski bus. It's unclear whether or not the Screwdriver helped me tighten up my skiing talents. But it sure made me a lot more fearless. And made skiing a lot more fun.

I never was, and never will be much of a downhill skier. But I found my niche in skiing. I discovered that I loved the bumps or "moguls" scattered throughout the slopes, that everyone else seemed to detest.

I found that if I would crouch down and then push off when I hit the crest of the mogul, I would fly through the air with the greatest of ease. For a few exhilarating feet.

The flying part of skiing was thrilling. The landings were sometimes not so good.

But with a little vodka in your belly you just kind of roll with the falls. And never once did I have to be helped down the hill, strapped into a ski patrol emergency sled.

Many years later I went skiing with Glenn Schmaltz, the bass player from my rock band, Mildstone.

"Come on Sweeney...Keep up with me!" he kept coaxing.

After a couple runs, Glenn and I stopped into the Lodge for a drink. We had a few "Coffee Nudges" and after we finished, I was good to go.

Determined to keep up this time, I threw all my vast knowledge from years of ski instruction out the window. I just watched Schmaltz, and tried to copy whatever he did.

Maybe the booze sped me up. Or maybe it slowed him down. Probably, it was a little bit of each. But this time, I was able to pretty much kept up with him. I didn't fall at all, and had the best time ever skiing.

I guess a little "Nudge" was all that I needed, to find my inner Jean Claude Sweeney.

18

THE TUKWILA TIGERS

I was far from the most athletic kid in my school. In fact, I was probably the slowest runner. In basketball it's well known that white men can't jump. But fat white kids like me. could barely make it off the ground at all.

No one is surprised to hear about the rabbits and squirrels romping in the woods in the land of the Hazelnuts. It fits. Salamanders, frogs and garter snakes? Of course. But Tigers prowling among the Hazelnut trees?

It's true. Tigers did roam the grounds of Tukwila Elementary School. That was the name of our School Team. And believe it or not, I was a Tiger too. Not a very ferocious one, but a tiger nonetheless.

I tried out for the basketball team. I'm sure our coach, Mr. Little, who was fittingly, a small, short man (with a large mouth) had experienced his own share of teasing as he was growing up. Because he really rallied the team, to embrace the nickname that he had chosen for me.

"Big Sweeney, with the little Weenie" got laughs from everyone, including myself. Shucks, it was sort of funny, for the moment.

But I had no idea my descriptive nickname was going to endure for years to come.

We had some great natural talent on Tukwila Elementary hoop team. Like our towering tall guy, Brad Sterling, And our all-around sports champion, Rusty Trudeau. Even my old wrestling sparring buddy, George Howard was an athletic asset to the Tiger pride.

For me, it was hard to compete when you couldn't run, jump or shoot. Sure, I could dribble. But only when I was taking a drink from the water fountain. So, spent most of my time polishing the bench with my gym shorts. While my teammates raced around the gym making shots and scoring points.

I never even attempted to get on the school's baseball team. But I would play at lunch and recess. Unlike it was choosing players for a tug of war, I was always the last man picked. By default, when all the decent players had already been drafted.

It was pretty "far out". I would end up in far, FAR left field. Probably as a secondary backup to the primary left fielder.

Yes, I was, outstanding in my field. My spot was not far from the Jasperson's apple orchard that bordered the school fence.

I must have been a mile away from the diamond. Baseballs NEVER made it this far out. So I would sometimes venture over the fence for a snack from Jasperson's trees while the guys were busy with an endless inning in the infield.

It might have been Barry Long, (ironically was one of the SHORTEST kids in our class) who one day smacked the ball out to my uncharted region of the baseball field. Just as I was returning from the fruit trees. I dropped my apple in favor of the ball.

Then everyone discovered something about my baseball talents. Even if the ball came right to me, I wasn't a very good catch.

Having blown my big chance, I might have redeemed myself if I picked up my dropped ball, and sent it sailing to home plate for the out.

But we learned even more about my baseball skills. I couldn't throw much better than the girls who were laughing at me from the sidelines either.

I'm sure that everyone thought I would be better at the dinner plate, than at home plate. But when I stepped up to bat, I surprised everyone including myself when I hit the ball a country mile.

I think it landed somewhere near the apple core I had dropped in left field. It should have been a homer, but since I was such a sluggish runner, the outfielder scrambled and threw the ball to the second baseman, who tagged me out.

Once I discovered I could hit, I felt like a little Babe Ruth, rather than a clumsy Baby Huey. I couldn't field to save my life, but at the plate, everyone agreed, I was a real swinger.

So, as I rose in celebrity, I tried to add a little style to my performance at the plate.

I would strut up, choking my bat, smiling at all the spectators, and eyeball the pitcher ready to pick off even a bad pitch and send the ball off to kingdom come.

But my signature swing was following through and letting my bat fly though the air as I waddled on off to first base for my single.

I thought that it looked cool, and so did everyone else. Until the time I tossed my bat and the spinning wooden missile smacked a poor little girl square in the forehead, and knocked her out cold.

Later that day. in tears, I was being scolded by principal Larry Snowden in the office.

"You could have killed her" he said frankly. "You gave her a pretty bad concussion"

I was almost hysterical. Yes, I had longed to finally be "a somebody" on the baseball field. But not at the expense of killing the fans.

I seldom touched the bat again. And when I did, I swore that I would never throw my bat, as long as I would live.

My Dad was a football player in High School, and considering my physique and limited running abilities, he suggested I try out for to be a lineman. Who knows? Maybe he meant a lineman to work on the telephone poles. But I thought he meant on Tukwila's football team.

In grade school we had an Flag Football Team that competed against the other elementary schools in our district.

I proudly wore the jersey of a Tiger and held my position as a guard.Since it wasn't tackle football, no one ever got badly hurt as far as I remember.

The quarterbacks, Joe Aliment, and later Rusty Trudeau and any other potential receivers all wore red flags that were partially tucked into their pants and both sides. What was considered a tackle was to pull out their flags.

It was kind of a pacifist's way of playing a brutal game.

"Oh, you tackled me, darn it! Now give me my flags back!"

So, on the bench, they would be eating ham sandwiches, not nursing torn hamstrings. At least for the running backs.

But on the line where I lived, it was a full contact sport.

My job was to protect Joe or Rusty from the opponents who

were determined to pull the flags out of their britches. So, we lineman would bash into each other full force, with no pads.

We were the human equivalents of doormats, who would get stomped on to keep from getting dirt on our quarterback's nice carpet.

Regarding the other guards that I faced around the league, none of them scared me in the least. The only one I feared, was a guy on our own team.

During practices, I would usually face up against either George Howard or John Howat. In football, George and I were closely matched at the time. He had the height and speed advantage over me, but I had weight and inertia on my side.

But John Howat was like a Mack Truck. And of course, I was the flimsy barricade on the road to the quarterback.

Not on some, but on every play, at the snap John would turn into a runaway locomotive, and the next thing I knew, I'd be laid out flat.

Rather than me blocking him, putting me against Howat was like laying out a red carpet directly to the quarterback. If he didn't either hand off or pass when it was my job to block John, the quarterbacks might as well kiss their flags goodbye.

I don't know how well George fared against John. I was too busy trying to find the wind that Howat knocked out of me to notice how anyone else was doing. But I know John built up quite a reputation around the district as the flagman of Tukwila.

For me, there was no Heisman Trophy in my future. I retired from school sports at the end of the Sixth grade.

I don't know if they even made Letterman jackets in my size. But needless to say, I never got the opportunity to wear one.

I know that today, all of the kids are a rewarded for just trying in sports. I don't completely agree with that philosophy. The real world is a very competitive place, and I think children need to be taught that there are winners and losers. Not everyone is gifted at everything.

A kid in my situation could and should consider his options when he discovers that his performance is subpar.

They can either work their tails off and improve or find something else that is more suited to their particular aptitudes.

In grade school, I recognized early that I was probably never going to become a jock, or get a free ride at the University of Washington on a basketball scholarship. Or even in baseball.

Later in High School, I found a sport that I was pretty good at. Playing pinball at the "Riverton Heights Ice Creamery and Delicatessen"

Howard, who ran the "Deli" as we called it, was a good guy. He was probably about 55 years old, but from his height, you would guess he was in 6th grade.

With his short crew cut and graying hair, he looked like he could have been Mr. Weber's brother. But he was always friendly to the kids who came to get treats, goodies or sundaes from his old-style soda fountain counter.

Occasionally he'd tell us to knock it off if we got too rowdy. But Howard had hired a crabby old lady with a piercing voice to keep the kids in order for routine noisiness.

Lon and I spent so much time up there, I'm surprised that Howard didn't give us gold watches when we graduated and essentially retired from pinball.

But my ONLY High School sports "Glory Days" were spent at

the Pinball Machines at Howard's.

There was never really any future in the playing the Silver ball, but Lon and I ranked right behind the pinball wizard extraordinaire, Tommy in the international standings.

Howard's was a great place to develop our flipper fingers. I must admit though, I always played second fiddle to Shank.

Lon could make the ball do anything that he wanted it to do. And he would nearly "turn over" the points counter with his high scores. Through intensive experimentation, Lon also knew where to give the machines a good smack, so they would spit out free games.

I would often watch Lon to learn his tricks. Like how to trap the ball on my flipper to prepare for a "bonus" shot. Or observing what part of the flipper would launch my ball into the spot on the bumpers where it was just sit there bouncing back and forth, chalking up thousands of points.

The best thing about choosing Howards as our pinball palace, was they had the perfect fuel for playing this demanding sport. They made the world's best Banana splits and Sundaes.

None of that imitation "soft serve", splashed with a thin, runny syrup and nondairy cool whip on top that you find in the "chain restaurants".

These splits had 3 scoops of rich, hardcore hand packed Chocolate, Strawberry and Vanilla. With gooey hot fudge, sugar fortified strawberry and Pineapple sauces drowning the ice cream and bananas.

Buried in a mountain range of real whipped cream with big peaks and valleys. And topped off with a hailstorm of pralines on the snow white whipped cream, and 3 cherries to crest each mound of the ice cream.

These Banana Splits helped make me into the man that I am today. I'm not bragging, I'm just saying.

As a sport town, Seattle was not really on the map back in those days. Yes we had the Sonics. But no NFL football team until the Seahawks debuted in the late 70s.

We did have REAL baseball however, and it made some of my fondest memories with my Dad.

It was a SICK man who brought baseball, as I knew it to Seattle.

Before Safeco, before even the Kingdome, before the Mariners, even before the Pilots, Emil Sick's Stadium defined for me what the game of baseball was all about.

In open-air bleachers with fly balls shooting through the skies and bags of peanuts sailing through the stands, baseball had a whole different swing to it. Rainers ball seemed so much more organic than either in Safeco or the Kingdome.

Sicks Stadium had wooden fences with painted advertisements and knotholes for peeking through surrounding the outfield. While it was a pretty good-sized park, Sicks Stadium seemed intimate. I felt more a part of the game. than I do watching the Mariners in Safeco.

You could see the color of the pitcher's snoose on the native dirt. And the blades of worn grass around his mound. You could even see and hear the reactions of the players in the dugouts without cameras.Maybe we just had better seats. And or, better eyes and ears then.

It didn't matter that the Rainers were minor league. It was still major league fun for us. "Root, toot tooting for the home team" Sons and Dads spent the innings together, heckling the away team batters, and cheering for our own.

And occasionally Dad might even share a sip of his beer with you. What the heck. This WAS Emil Sick's house and he was the owner of the Rainer Brewery.

We had such a good time there, that we didn't "care if we if we never got back"

But as Seattle baseball took on a Hollywood glitter in ritzy new digs, a new Lowe's store rose from the dust of our favorite old ball park. And baseball would never be quite the same, at least for me.

While I carry many great memories of the Rainers in Sicks Stadium around in my mind, I sure wish that I could carry a few of the baseball cards from my bubble gum in my pocket. If so, I'd be a wealthy man today.

19

LOST FORTUNES

We all could have been millionaires today, if we had played our cards right. As we were growing up, the highways were jammed with classic cars from the 50s and 60s, that are now seen at car shows, costing 6 digits.

By the time we got our licenses, any kid with a part time job could pick up one of those now expensive cars dirt cheap. If we had only kept our first couple of cars, we would have been able to retire in splendor on the proceeds.

Those Mickey Mantle, Johnny Bench, or Nolan Ryan baseball cards that cost the price of a stick of gum, often ended up as noisemakers in the spokes of our bicycles. A dozen or so of those choice collectibles would put us behind the wheels of Lamborghinis today.

My own stack of 10 cent Superman and Batman comics would ring up at hundreds of dollars apiece today. But as my interest in them began to wane, Mom would be anxious to put that clutter in the trash. My comic book goldmine is now rotting in a landfill somewhere. Thanks Mom.

But she didn't know what their value would eventually become. Nor did I.

I treasured my yellow Mickey Mouse School Bus lunchbox in early elementary school. By the time I hit my teens, I couldn't have cared less about the Goofy thing. But if I wanted to buy one today from an antique store, they are priced like they were made of solid gold.

No one realized that our toy boxes were literal Fort Knox's back in the day. But looking at eBay, it's obvious that the toy hoarders don't need a 401K plan to finance their golden years.

Just a few choice Golden Books, your sister's Barbie Doll, and a shoe box full of Hot Wheels cars would make a nice start on a nest egg. I recently saw a Jimi Hendrix poster that was originally given out for free at a concert, going for $10,000. Whoa! 'Scuse me, while I kiss the sky...!'

Those also, got thrown out.

I grieve over the fortunes that we threw away unwittingly. But at the same time, the memories of growing up with those mementos of the era, PRICELESS....

An old Beatles album in excellent condition may fetch a lot of money if you're willing to part with it. But if you were lucky enough to have experienced being in the coliseum watching them on their first tour, those things just can't be bought.

You can buy a blue ray of the entire Star Wars series, remastered for under $100. But you can't recreate the excitement of standing in lineall the way around the block of the Cinerama, in the rain, to see the original Star Wars premiere. At any price. It was a real event, not just another night at the movies.

Even the sad events like the Kennedy Assassination have been viewed millions of times on YouTube. But the video cannot capture the anguish, shock and mourning that we all shared, witnessing it live. We all remember where we were, and what we were doing on that sad day.

If we had played it smart, we could have had the treasures of living in those times, and the substantial value of the antiques that we bought fresh and new to cash in today. But who knew then we were filling our trash cans with gold? It does make a strong case for hoarding however.

As Joni Mitchell sang, "Don't it always seem to go, that you don't know what you've got 'till it's gone?"

Regardless of the monetary value, there are many things from the 60s that I wish we had never disposed of. One would be the community spirit, of neighbors knowing one another, and looking out for each other.

If you didn't lock your house, it would most likely be found intact when you returned home. And if you left your keys in the car, it wouldn't go anyplace until you returned and sat once again behind your wheel. There was a trust and safety, worth more than any of our possessions.

I also would have kept the pride in the American way, and Yankee ingenuity that we were famous for. Most everyone realized what a great country and a great city we lived in. Americans were unstoppable in our innovations and industries. And rewarded for it in our standard of living.

When companies prospered, the workers shared in the harvest. Made in America was the Good Housekeeping Seal of Approval, throughout the globe. We all stood and saluted the flag, realizing that the life in America was good and getting better all the time.

20

PLACES TO GO, THINGS TO DO

It's probably better for the beasts nowadays, but Woodland Park Zoo in the 1960s was designed to let the kids get up close and personal to the animals. Whether the animals liked it or not.

There were few hiding places for many of the zoo residents to get away from the crowds. Every day was an open house at the zoo. In today's Woodland Park, they have built natural habitats, and secluded areas for the animal's privacy and isolation. At least for the Lions and Gorillas, they can decide whether or not they are ready to have company. You may or may not get to see them. Not then.

Maybe that's why our celebrity Gorilla, Bobo used to angrily pound on the glass. It would shock and terrify the children at first. Then the kids would laugh, realizing that they were safe behind the Gorilla's glass window, inches thick.

He would beat his chest and scowl at the visitors. Bobo wasn't a very congenial host. He would touch himself inappropriately and jam his finger up his nose without ever hesitating to consider his manners.

"Hey! If you don't like it, you want to DO something about it?" he seemed to say. No one would have dared if they could have.

Indeed, Bobo was one tough customer. But he probably was gay. Repeated attempts to get him to breed with the female Gorilla Fifi were unsuccessful. Fifi often cried herself to sleep at night.

Maybe some candlelight and champagne would have helped set the mood. But Bobo probably would have busted the bottle against the glass, and used the candle to torch the place.

The Bears on the other hand, loved to interact with the kids. Surely, they would have rather had a drumstick from one of the children's arms to gnaw on. But in lieu, they were happy to stand up to beg and perform for the peanuts that we would toss them.

Feeding the animals wasn't prohibited. It was accepted, and even encouraged. They sold peanuts in kiosks around the park, for that expressed purpose.

Every kid could feel like a VIP with the "key to the city", if their parents would spring for a "Zoo-Key". These were little plastic elephants; whose trunks formed a key that would activate a narration for each exhibit.

While we might not stick around to hear the whole spiel, it was "neat", that we were given the power and control to make those educational speeches happen, at will.

Going to the Zoo was an interesting, affordable and fun way to spend the day. Whether with your family or on a class field trip. I've returned to Woodland Park in the last couple years and it's changed dramatically.

It's hard to find the animals. There is no feeding allowed. And the prices are ridiculous. Even if they still offered the Zoo-Keys, after paying admission, we probably couldn't afford one.

Another of my favorites was the Pacific Science Center.

Left over from the 1962 Seattle World's Fair, The Science Center is surrounded by its distinctive white arches, and pools of water. People would toss coins into the shallow waters. To a kid, it looked like millions of dollars in copper and silver lining the bottom. We wished we could be the pool cleaners.

And inside, seeing the exhibits were worth a million bucks to an excited kid. They were mostly hands on, interactive displays. We dashed from one fascinating exhibit to the next.

My personal favorite was the space exhibit. Space travel was a big subject in the 1960s, and astronauts were like rock stars. What could be more thrilling to an 8-year-old than climbing aboard a replica of a Gemini space capsule? Nothing in THIS world.

Traveling to the Seattle Center, which housed the Science center was easy and safe for little kids, even without Mom and Dad, thanks to the bus.

Before Metro, or King County Transit, Tukwila was connected to Seattle by Greyhound buses. They would stop down by the Locke's Tukwila Store and if you were around 10 years old, you were old enough to ride alone or with your friends.

It was always a big adventure going into town. Even before I was old enough to ride solo on the bus, my older sister Linda would sometimes take me with her. I'd tag along as she shopped the stores, but what I really loved was stopping at the soda fountain at Bartell's for lunch and a "Green River". That's the only place I've ever had that beverage.

They had a real soda jerk preparing the drinks, and little red round stools that a restless boy could spin around on until he got good and dizzy.

In downtown Seattle, they had their City Transit electric trolleys, powered by the tangled cobwebs of high voltage power lines overhead. As the buses oscillating arms would skip over the wires, they would snap, crackle, and pop Lightning bolts of arcing voltage flashed in the streets, like it was on the night that Frankenstein's monster came to life.

Kind of creepy, but cool.

Once downtown, I loved to stop in at Meyer's Music and look at all the guitars, amplifiers wah wah pedals, and fuzz face effects boxes. My buddies and I would also check out the flashing lights advertising the "peep shows", trying to imagine what happened inside those forbidden doors.

We would meander through the streets, eventually finding our way to the Monorail. Our hearts would begin to beat faster as we neared the Seattle Center.

First things first. We ran from the Monorail landing to buy a handful of tickets for the rides. Smiling, laughing, sometimes puking, we rode them all. The good ones twice.

The Wild mouse with its hairpin turns, the Flight to Mars, the upside-down fun of the Rock-O-Plane. It wasn't Disneyland, but it was the closest thing that we had around here.

Then, loading up with carnival food like Cotton Candy and Hot Dogs, we would go pop balloons, try to knock off milk bottles with baseballs, do the shooting gallery and leave with a stuffed animal or two.

Next, the Arcade. There weren't any video games yet but there were a bunch of machines to test your strength. Or press a penny flat and emboss it with Seattle Center logos. Even test your intelligence.

We rode the Bubbleator, a round Plexiglas elevator up to the second floor of the Center House where we'd stop into the "Freak

Show" They had pictures and stories of bearded ladies, Siamese twins, the tallest, fattest, and skinniest people in the world.

Inside also were real Mummies, and a little automated encased puppet show of Judy Garland singing, "Somewhere Over the Rainbow". Every weird thing that would fascinate all us weird little kids.

Time and money permitting, we might take in the Science Center too before returning to the bus station for our ride back home.

As we would travel into Seattle in the mornings, our fellow riders were mostly other kids or little old ladies going into town to shop. Along with businessmen commuting to work. Moms were at home, and Dads were at work. But there was a different crowd on our return trips in the late afternoon.

By that time, all the winos and strange people would have rolled out of bed, and climbed aboard the Greyhound.

It seemed every bus had a token drunk, and a guy who talked to himself.

These days, you see lots of people talking into their Bluetooth. But these guys didn't have blue-teeth. Theirs were yellow or missing. They were having interesting, lively, conversations with themselves on each bus run. You didn't see as many of them on the streets then, as you do now. That's because they were all on the buses.

Along the way back home, you'd be talking to your friends, recounting the days fun and planning your next trip into town. At some point, the drunk guy would take an interest in one of us.

Telling him what a good boy he was. How he wished he could have a kid like him. And how he'd like to take him home. I didn't realize how creepy that was until years later.

But as we pulled up to our stop at Tukwila Store, we'd say goodbye to the drunk guy as the guy talking to himself rambled on. After a quick stop into the store for a Twinkie for our long walk home, we'd climb the hill.

Just in time for dinner.

21

I CAN HEAR MUSIC

Few of us turned out to be the Firemen, Astronauts, or Presidents that we imagined we would be when we finally became adults. As children in middle class America in the 60s, we each had our own dreams of what we might become when we grew up. In our idealistic little minds, there seemed to be no limits to where we might land if we were to put our minds to it.

If everything had worked out as I had planned at 7 years old, I would have probably become famous for at least one of my many high-profile careers. I thought I'd become a Doctor, working my way through school starring as an actor and stunt man in Oscar and Emmy winning movies and TV shows.

I especially relished the thought of being the stunt man. I loved to pretend that I had been shot and developed a very dramatic exit from this world. Tumbling to the ground, writhing in pain, quivering as the blood poured out of me.

Until I would finally release my soul, motionless with my outstretched arms reaching for heaven. Although I lived to die in an imagined Hollywood set, I was terrified of dying.

But when I hit 8 years old all my medical and theatrical ambitions took a backseat to my new career goal, inspired by a performance on the Ed Sullivan television show. After I saw them standing there singing "I want to Hold your happy little hands" and I watched the crowd go insane, I knew I wanted to be a ROCK STAR. Like the Beatles.

The fact that I couldn't sing, or play an instrument seemed like a minor insignificant detail. Whatever a kid could conceive and believe, he could achieve. So, I thought. It's odd, but it seemed the more we liked something, the worse our parents hated it. And there was not a subject where this was truer than in music.

Especially if we wanted to PLAY that "noise" as they called it.

My parents, in fact all parents hated the Beatles. But I loved their beat, loved their enthusiasm, their clever melodies and lyrics. I saw the joy they experienced while performing and the joy they brought their fans as they played.

I wanted to let my hair grow long and make the girls scream and faint too. It seemed like a good way to make a living.

I ran the numbers in my eager little mind. Would I rather spend an eternity in school, to learn how to listen to a heartbeat through a stethoscope? Or drop out of school, strap on an electric guitar and cause the hearts of adoring fans to beat with the rhythm of my music?

Would I rather have a prestigious degree hanging on my wall as I handed people their appendixes for thousands of dollars? Or live the prestigious life of signing autographs as people handed me their own hearts for millions of dollars?

Rather than heading to the operating rooms, I figured I needed to start grooming for fame and fortune, STAT. Not having an instrument, I began to work on my English accent that very night. And stared at the mirror impatiently waiting for my hair to grow long.

Although I did pursue a music career after high school, I made my fortune working in convenience stores, oiling machinery, driving forklifts and scaring the heck out of everybody operating cranes. The only riches I got from music was enriching my life.

But the music of the 60s did and still does deserve a full chapter in both our lives, and in this book.

From the Renaissance days to modern hip hop, I can't think of a more creative and inspired time for music than the 1960s.

In the laboratories of the recording studios in that decade, thousands of new genres came to life in hundreds of different musical flavors. It was a true melting pot of styles.

The cauldron was just beginning to boil in the 1950s as Bill Haley, Elvis Presley, Jerry Lee Lewis, and Little Richard stirred big band, country, gospel and blues together to crystallize into new Rockabilly and Boogie Woogie sounds that mankind had never heard before.

Meanwhile the crooners were having their voices buoyed by counterpoint harmonies and new rhythms that had never shared the same songs, in the land of Do Wop.

These early departures from traditional music poured the footings of the skyscrapers of pop music in the 60s and beyond. They had finally captured the attitude and energy of young people, as they danced through the joys and struggles of life.

But it wasn't until the Beatles turned the music up, and on its side that the rock really started rolling. One good idea would spawn another and soon radio speakers would provide a perfect backdrop for living in a world where the "times were always a changing"

It wasn't long after the lovable mop tops had plead for us to "Love me Do" that the darker and more rebellious Rolling Stones

146

began to complain that they just couldn't "Get No Satisfaction".

But regardless of what your musical tastes were, satisfaction was on its way as the British sound started to invade the American shores. The Dave Clarke Five were feeling "Glad all over", as the Animals moved into the "House of the Rising Sun" in New Orleans, and warned us "Not to do, as they had done"

Herman's Hermits soon came along. And something told us we were into "Something Good" Here in America, the Yankee ingenuity of Brian Wilson helped the Beach Boy's "Get around" in their fast cars racing down to the beaches for a little "Fun, Fun, Fun".

Not about to let those Brits win another revolution in music, Paul Revere and the Raiders came "Steppin' Out" with some real "Good Things" that made us "Hungry" for more.

And it was "Just like Me" to watch them host a daily TV show called "Where the Action Is" that kept us rocking' all week with a variety of new musical acts. Dick Clark kept the momentum going on the dance floor with his American Bandstand program.

Meanwhile the Beatles had bounced back with Rubber Souls and put in a "Hard Day's Night", trying to keep the English sound alive. The Stones had finally found their satisfaction with "Honky Tonk Women" and "Brown Sugar"

In Detroit, Smokey Robinson was making the Miracles happen in soul music, along with the Supremes, the Temptations, and the Four Tops, spinning on our record players. The Young Rascals started "Groovin'" from the Jersey Shores with their own "Blue Eyed" brand of soul. And it was the start of another "Beautiful Morning"

For the teeny boppers, Tommy James and the Shondells, Tommy Roe, and the Monkees were filling their hearts with song. And their walls with posters. And their own pockets with cash.

Folk music seemed to be on it's deathbed, until the Byrds, The Lovin' Spoonful, the Mama's and the Papas, and Bob Dylan traded in their dreadnoughts for electric 6 and 12 string guitars. And breathed new life into the once comatose style of music.

We all woke up to Psychedelic music when we heard the Strawberry Alarm Clock announce it was time to light up the "Incense and Peppermints"

The Box Tops begged that we "Give them a ticket for an Airplane", just as San Francisco's groups such as the Jefferson Airplane and the Grateful Dead were taking off.

About that time, Jim Morrison was opening the Doors down at the Whiskey a Go-Go and lighting the fire of another string of hot hits.

In the summer of love, Moby Grape was ripe for the pickin', and the Small Faces was wondering what will we do there in "Itchy-Coo Park"

Everyone knew it was "Windy", thanks to the Association. Steppenwolf stepped up with the harder edged, "Born to be Wild". Eric Clapton was giving us the Cream of the power trio crop with "Sunshine of your Love", and Hendrix was bursting on the scene in a "Purple Haze".

On the softer side, Glen Campbell was blending country with pop in "Galveston" and "Wichita Lineman" Lulu was singing "To Sir with Love" As a very young Stevie Wonder was testifying that he was, "Made to Love Her"

Just when you thought you knew the direction music was going, they would throw you a curve ball. Like Tiny Tim's "Tiptoe Through the Tulips" Or someone left your "Cake out in the Rain" at

"MacArthur's" Park" But, Tom Jones would remind us that it wasn't "Unusual" at all.

As the decade was coming to a close, southern and country rock were rising up from the swamps and the fields. With Creedence and the Allman Brothers, paving the path for Skynyrd and Molly Hatchet in the 70s.

But all this incredible variety of music highlighted the exciting times of our era, and provided an audio for the collage of our memories. The messages of love and good times attach themselves to my fondest memories. With crystal clear images, of times when "Yellow Submarines" ruled the seas, and Led Zeppelins floated through the skies.

The first notes of a song take me right back to where I was, and what I was doing, when I first heard it.

As "Brown Eyed Girl" kicks off, I find myself on Vacation with my Parents at Lake Coeur d'Alene. Watching unlimited Hydroplanes close up as, Van Morrison sang through my little transistor radio.

Hearing the "House of the Rising Sun" puts my first guitar back in my hands. And reminds me of the struggle to play an "F" chord for the first time.

We don't have time to go through my thousands of song and event associations, but I'm sure you have a few of your own. Mostly, they help us recall the times from our crazy youth, when we were carefree and all "Happy Together".

Many of us, inspired by our favorite groups and singers took a stab at making music ourselves. At Tukwila Elementary, our musical education began in the fourth grade.

The whole class had the pleasure of breaking into the music

"business, with a mandatory "song flute" class. We learned a "C" scale together, blowing our brains out on these cheap plastic instruments.

It was a terrible noise, that combined the discordant shrieks of an out of out of control violin, with the nasally squawks of a couple dozen parakeets on acid.

I'm sure Mrs. Wene thought, "this was a mistake", and scratched it from the curriculum for future classes.

I remember our first song, as out of time and out of tune as it was. We all played "Go tell Aunt Rhody" in unison. But we wouldn't need to tell Aunt Rhody to turn down her hearing aid.

Meanwhile, my parents had bought my brother and I, a couple cheap plastic guitars. Lon and I repeatedly broke mine, playing "El Kabong" inspired by a character on Quick Draw McGraw (No relation, as far as I know, to "Doctor Phil" McGraw)

But we not only learned a little about guitar, but also about welding. We would reattach the neck of my guitar using my "wood burning" iron.

Back in the classroom, the opportunity to join the school band had kids showing up with shiny new Bundy and Conn Trumpets, Selmer clarinets and Ludwig snare drums that their parents surely regretted.

Not thinking clearly, I chose a "real" flute. Mostly because my buddy Jeff Moore had gotten one. I soon learned the rest of the flute section were all girls. So, I quickly petitioned my folks to let me trade for the more "macho" trumpet

In Junior High, I switched over to the Baritone to further my music MAN image. But I stopped short of playing the Tuba, when I realized it's not the SIZE of your instrument so much as how you use it.

We learned some rudimentary music theory, and the basics of sight reading. But never was the grade school band "tight", or even pleasant to listen to.Nevertheless, the school held "concerts" to convince the parents their money was well spent on our instruments.

I'll bet many of the parents thought a barking, puppy peeing all over the carpet, would have been a quieter and less annoying investment.   But they politely gave us a round of forced applause after every number.

We didn't sell T shirts or posters at those shows. But the PTA made a few bucks selling home baked cookies on the gig nights.

The response we got at the school band concerts wasn't enough to give us false hopes making it in the music business. But I was still determined to make my mark on the Billboard charts in a Rock n Roll band.

My first band, named the "Panic Button", had Punky Summers playing drums (which were just big and little coffee cans) Mike Bergstrom on the upright piano, and me on the bad guitar.

We spent more time talking about making music and becoming stars than actually playing. Mike was kind of like Schroeder in the Charlie Brown comic strip. Well versed in Beethoven and Bach, but he didn't have a clue on how to rock.

Punky seemed to think the whole thing was kind of stupid. But I was pushing hard to get us heading in the right direction, for fortune and fame. I don't think the others embraced my dream.

But I finally got together with a couple of kids who really seemed to see the "big picture" of touring the world, making tons of money, and having fun as our songs played on radios throughout the world.

Mark Emberg was the Pastor's son, whom I had met at Church

Camp. As a clergyman's son, you'd think he would have been a saintly, altar boy, but he was far from that. He had more rock n roll sensibility than anyone I had met.

He was one of the first kids I'd ever seen smoking a cigarette. He cussed like a sailor. But he could play the guitar like a ring in a bell. He could sing too.

Unlike Mark, Darby Gerking was a kid from my own school, and I'd known him ever since First grade. But I had no idea that he really knew how to play the drums. He even had a drum set, and could sing. I was thrilled to learn that He and Mark could harmonize too.

Mark was a child prodigy on guitar and he taught me lots of tricks. Mostly, I played bass by picking the lower strings on my guitar, while Mark played rhythm and lead. He was my mentor, and pretty much anything I played was under the direction of Mark.

Later in Jr High, we added Delbert Webster on bass and I switched to rhythm guitar. We played a gig at Mark's school, McKnight Middle school in Renton where Mark sang and called the shots. That went well.

But in seventh grade there was a talent show at Showalter (which had changed from a grade school to a Jr High) Mark wouldn't be allowed there, as you had to be a student to participate.

I was too shy to sing, and I think Darby had moved to the Highline School District. So, he wasn't able to perform with us either.   Delbert moved to the drums and became our singer by default.

He sang Creedence Clearwater Revival's, Susie Q. The odds of probability say that even tone-deaf Delbert should have accidentally hit the right pitch once in a while, just by default. Could have, should have...but he didn't.

He had beat the odds of landing off pitch on each note, and gave a vocal performance that would have made Simon Cowell vomit on his desk.

I think it had a little comedic appeal nevertheless. Delbert redeemed us a little, as we did a strictly instrumental rendition of "In a Gadda da Vidda" with its never-ending drum solo.

But we had real competition from some bad boys who had come from the Central School badlands.

Gary and Glenn Schmaltz, along with Dino Ullakko and Steve Tomaso, ruled that battle of the bands. My band bowed our heads in shame, after Schmaltz and company did a respectable performance. With Dino on the drums, Gary and Glenn on guitar and bass, respectively. And Steve, I don't remember what he did. He might have sung.

It wasn't fair, because the Schmaltz had been tutored by Dennis Capps, who lead our real local Rock Heroes, "The Magnetic Field"

The Magnetic Field, consisting of Dennis, his brother Albert, and Gary Sorrells rocked a number of parties and keggars around Tukwila. They truly amazed me.

Dennis had rock star charisma, a great voice and fingers that could play virtually anything. To this day, I can't figure out how they could pull off a layered orchestrated song like the Moody Blues, "Tuesday Afternoon", convincingly.

I think it had a lot to do with the extreme volume of their Altec Lansing "Voice of the Theater" sound horns. They would cause halls like "Thorndyke Community Hall" or "McMicken's" to rumble like a California earthquake was taking place.

After the reign of Magnetic Field, Dennis continued to make great music in a variety of bands performing around South Seattle.

A couple of years after graduation from High School, the Schmaltz brothers, Randy Brigham and I formed Mildstone. While we had a great time and high hopes, we never achieved the super stardom that we craved.

We still, as I'm sure you do, carry the melodies of those days etched indelibly in our minds. No matter where we went from there, the beat of that decade goes on.

Styles change over time, but the spirit of our music chronicled our era. Throughout the 60s and 70s, the prevalent themes of our songs were love, peace, happiness and fun.

Even our sad songs stirred up compassion and empathy for the heartbreaks and suffering they described. Beginning in the 1980s, and becoming more distinct over time, the groove of music has abandoned love, in favor of anger and angst.

Does the music reflect the times, or do the times inspire the music? Probably a little bit of each.

But no matter whether the beat is hip hop, or good old-fashioned rock' n ' roll, this would be my impossible dream. For us to reach out in the darkness and say, "Come on people now, smile on your brother, everybody get together try to love one another right now."

22

OH, BROTHER!

We were impressionable as kids. And for good or bad, there were multiple influences that battled for position in our values. Our parents tried to lay out a moral fabric for us to stitch upon. While our friends would suggest many things that might create a stark contrast to those values.

While trying to decide who and what we should be, we were being drawn in opposite directions. The media, culture, music and the criterion for being "cool" were all factors. But often we would look to our older siblings for a balanced view of where we might fall between our emerging generation and the establishment. At least I did.

Similar to Wally Cleaver, my brother Tom and his friends were the guides who translated the idealistic wisdom and morals of my Mom and Dad, into the real-life challenges of living in a changing world.

And like the Beav, I valued his opinion and his understanding of how those principles worked out in the "real world".

I respected the sincerity and good sense of the virtues my parents were preaching. But I looked to my brother to gauge the relevance of their credos in the 60s. Times had changed since the 20s and 30s when Mom and Dad grew up.

It's no big revelation that little brothers can be pests, and I was no exception. Most of the time when I was a child, he didn't want me hanging around. Not because he thought that I would "rat him out".

I'd learned early that squealing on him didn't earn me many brownie points with Mom. But instead he would get off the hook, and I'd be reprimanded for tattling. But little brothers were just "uncool", and I was told to "scram" much more often than I was invited to tag along with Tom. Especially when he was with his friends.

My motive was to see how he operated and let some of his "cool" rub off on me. Since I wasn't welcome in his circle of friends, I had to learn much of this from a distance, by observation.

Tom not only taught me the cool things that I should gravitate towards, he also taught me the dangers to stay away from. As a very young boy, Tom warned me about Dragonflies.

"They'll sew your lips together" he cautioned, with a hint of a smile.

I didn't see what was so funny. With thief long needle like abdomens, it was plausible they could do a pretty tidy stitch on a kid's face.

I shuddered as I watched one of those colorful insect seamstresses zip by us. I ran faster than a fat boy should have been able to!

Once safely inside my house, I caught my breath and sighed. Having dodged this bullet. I had reservations about ever going outside again.

It wasn't until years later, when I checked in the World Book

Encyclopedia, that the Dragonfly myth was busted. Yet to this day, I still cringe a little when I hear their flutter. Hysteria is slow to die.

Yet he did alleviate my phobia about furniture tags. In an official, serious stern font, furniture and pillows were marked with a tag that threatened, "DO NOT REMOVE...under PENALTY of the LAW".

"Oh NO!" I thought. "I've seen it! I've even held the tag in my HAND! What if it falls OFF?!? What if somebody SAW me?!?!?"

I imagined screaming sirens, and red flashing lights (they hadn't invented BLUE police lights yet) coming up the driveway. A squad of officers would surround me, guns drawn. And haul me off to the pokey....

I told my brother about my worries, panting with fear.

After a good laugh he explained, "That's only for the STORES. Take it easy...."

Whew! Even if the tag did somehow get removed, I would be acquitted. Case dismissed.

As time passed and he neared the end of high school and got into college, he became more accepting of me. I think there were two related factor that facilitated this change of heart.

First, I had become cooler over the years. And secondly, I don't think he put quite as high of a premium on showing how cool he was as peer pressure diminished and the worth of blood relations grew in his assessment.

For Tom, it had started out rocky with me. Being the 3rd kid in our family behind my two sisters he had savored all of the "last child" perks up until my arrival. At 5 years old, I don't think he liked me pushing him to the middle of the pack.

Nevertheless, learning that he would soon be having a little brother soon, brought up all kinds of ideals of having his own personal little buddy to play with. Boy, did I let him down. The sight of seeing me wearing a hospital bracelet left him disillusioned from the start.

"What a sissy" he thought. "Bracelet...I thought I was getting a little brother, not a sister" And the sight of me sucking my thumb. "Oh Brother" he balked.

Tom was on the cutting edge of cool. Just when I thought I was being hip, he would out hip me. When I got my first Beatle record, he had gone on to the Stones.

I'd sneak in his room and listen to The Turtles, and he'd come home with Moby Grape. I'd think I was really happening with my AM radio tuned into KJR's top 40. And he'd be twisting the dial to KOL FM's underground rock. As I was drinking my first beer with my friends, Tom was firing up his first joint with his.

But to my benefit, Tom was a trailblazer for breaking in Mom and Dad. When it came to alcohol or marijuana, his experimentation was shock and awe to our parents.

By the time I rolled around to trying these it was old hat. "Boys will be boys" they figured and since Tom had come out okay, they figured I would probably work through the phases without any permanent damage as well. Neither of their boys turned out to be drug addicts or alcoholics.

It wasn't easy living in his shadow however. As my pals and I were gawking at the lingerie ads in the Penney's catalog, Tom and his friends were making out with real girls. When I was hiking through the woods with my Boy Scout troop, Tom was bombing around town in his first car. And as I was just getting started in Jr High, he was a senior driving around in an extra cool 58 retractable hardtop Ford.

How cool is that?

When I finally got to grow my hair out fashionably long, he was sporting sideburns. As I was delivering newspapers, he was getting his first real paying jobs. I just couldn't keep up with his cool. I couldn't get a single whisker to grow at the time.

Meanwhile, I continued to be a little brother sized thorn in his side. For instance, I would sometimes run a little short on my allowance money, but I knew where all his stashes were in his bedroom.

In a drawer below his sliding closet, he had a little box with quite a bit of change in it. I wasn't stealing, but I would use it as a bank to give myself a little payday loan. I had every intention of paying him back when I ever got ahead.

Little did I know that the box was filled with rare coins he had collected while doing his paper route, and the quarter I would later replace was actually an irreplaceable mint error or valuable old coin. I gave Frank's Fixit shop many dollars in collectibles in exchange for Nickel and Dime candies. If I'd had a little brother like myself, I probably would have wished that I had been an only son too.

Lon's older brother Allen had a collection of coins too that Lon raided. These were foreign however, not American. But Lon realized that the Mexican Centavo which was worth less than a penny was the same size and thickness as an American Quarter. The pinball machine thought it was close enough, and we played many games for only a few pennies. They also worked sweetly in candy and pop machines.

I had a great idea. I told Lon we should go to Mexico and trade in our dollars for centavos and then exchange them back in change machines for real nickels and dimes. I didn't really see it as being an ethical issue. It was just taking advantage of a flaw in the system.

A fundamental business principle. Buy low and sell high. Before we actually carried out the scheme, I thought better of both the morality and the legality of our caper.

I'm happy that I saw the light before stepping into felonious territory, irrespective of how profitable it might have been. It would have been tough to tell the killers in the next prison cell that we were in for cashing in centavos.

As Tom went off to college and got his own pad, he softened on his opinion of me. He even used to invite me to visit and hang out sometimes. And he continued to influence me. A high school kid could learn a lot about cool from a college guy. But he also shared a lot of philosophy with me. He stressed the importance of honesty and the merits of your word.

Tom was also one of my early driving instructors. He retired from that job after I blasted through two red lights and one stop sign. But he did risk his life trying to show me the rules of the road. I don't think he's ever been a passenger in my car since. Not that I blame him.

I'm shocked to discover that kids like my nieces and nephews aren't as excited about learning to drive as we were.

After becoming a teenager, no other upcoming event in our lives had as much allure as getting behind the wheel.

When I learned to drive, cars were twice as big as they are now. They guzzled gas and when the speed limit was 70, everyone cheesed a little and cruised at 80 to 85. But it was easy to tell where you were going back then, even by smell.

23

NOSING YOUR WAY AROUND TOWN

Long before GPS, even blindfolded Tukwila drivers could have navigated around Puget Sound guided simply by their senses of hearing and smell.

If the sulfur odors were getting stronger and stronger, you had to be heading south toward the "Aroma of Tacoma" from its pulp mills.

When someone said, "Pew...That smells like a DEAD HORSE", Obviously you are heading east toward the Rendering Works, where they were busy cooking up hot pot of glue for you.

The sound of traffic, the blare of car horns, and the noise of an occasional car crash, let you know you were heading west, closing in on I-5.

When you heard the rumble of jet airplanes, you knew you were nearing the runways of Sea Tac Airport.

Planes really made their presence known in the days before turbojets were replaced by turbofans. The houses would shake as travelers flew the "Noisy Skies" of United.

If you could smell the sea breezes, you were obviously heading west toward Puget Sound. Fresh, and stale fish odors meant you were likely around Pike Place Market.

Once you started getting whiffs of French fries and bird droppings, you must be close to Ivar's Fish Bar.

Seagulls did then and still do amazing stunt flying to compete for greasy fingers of potatoes, until they ultimately die from strokes and coronaries brought on by their high cholesterol diets.

The scent of industrial smoke, let you know you were close to the smokestacks from the steel mills and factories in South Seattle.

As the flavor of the smoke became sweeter, you might be drawing near the marijuana fumes from the Frat Houses in the "U district" Or if it smelled a bit skunky, you were either taking in the scent of some bad weed, or else you had drifted over to the Cascade foothills and had run over a black and white polecat.

The smell of fresh cow manure wafting into your nostrils would tell you that you were somewhere in the Kent Valley, perhaps near Smith Brother's farm. Or if it left a Rhino or Elephant aftertaste in your mouth, you could have been passing by Woodland Park Zoo.

But if you kept your eyes open, you could often see Mount Rainier popping up on the horizon like an inviting scoop of ice cream from the observation deck of the Space Needle.

And in midsummer, the roar of unlimited hydroplanes would echo all through Tukwila and the Kent Valley as the Thunder boats roared around Lake Washington.

Pat O'Day rallied the whole city's excitement as the boats thundered in the lake and the Blue Angels soared overhead. They still race, albeit more quietly and without the razzmatazz they aroused in the 60s.

There was so much to see, smell and hear in the Seattle area in the 1960s. While there still is, the views seem more obstructed, and most of those familiar sounds have been muffled and subdued. And the smells have been "Fabreeze-ed" away, to the point where you pretty much have to drive with your eyes open anymore.

24

HOT WHEELS

Certainly, the 60s and the 70s were "Happy Days". But for me and most of my friends, the happiest day of all was the day we got our driver's licenses. I'd been revving and warming up the motor of my mind for years dreaming about getting on the road. Freedom was a tank of gas and keys to the car.

Along with singing the praises of surfing and the beaches, the Beach Boys next favorite subject was cars. The independence that came from driving was central to almost any brand of "Fun, Fun, Fun" that a teenager was looking for.

Some of the richer kids were given cars by their parents. But many of us had to work for our wheels. Some took after school jobs. My deal was that I had to paint our house, and in exchange the parents would pay for my pricey car insurance.

And so far as owning my own car, Dad gave me his cherished 65 LTD that he had bought new, as my graduation present. I was surprised that he would relinquish it to me, but on the other hand, I had accidentally "customized" it earlier by running the right quarter panel into a concrete post.

Knowing my Dad's Irish temper, I thought he would have flipped out when I told him about the damage. But he was amazingly calm and understanding.

"Oh well" he said. "Things happen. Just be more careful from now on" was his response. But from that time, he seemed less enthusiastic about his pride and joy car. It was marred. He had an excuse to buy himself a newer updated LTD. And it paved the way for me getting the 65 for keeps for finishing High School.

I don't know why, but four doors weren't cool among my collection of friends. Galaxies and the Plymouth Furys were among the most "square" cars at the time. I didn't care. I wasn't a big car buff. It was a great car to get me around in.

But a lot of guys sported. "Dual Quads", "Glass Packs" "Cragars" and having "Big Meats" as tires. These were some of the features that would make your car stand out. I didn't really want to race. I just wanted to "cruise" with my favorite songs cued up on my 8-track tape player.

It was hip to "burn 'em off" and "pop your clutch" but I drove an automatic with no clutch and horsing around on the road meant much less to me that the privilege of driving meant.

That's because Dad had warned, "If I see or hear about you 'Hot Rodding', you're done" I knew he meant it.

So as tempting as it would be to make my tires squeal and bomb around in the car... Dad's threat combined with Mom's all seeing "little bird" to turn me in kept me on the straight and narrow road.

While I wasn't about to go speeding or hot rodding at the expense of my driving privileges, my buddy Lon wasn't under such scrutiny. So, I had a blast bombing around town with him in his early 60s Falcon.

It could barely "burn 'em off" on pavement. But he made more donuts than "Dunkins" in the parking lot of St. Thomas Church on a snowy day.

Later, Shankel got a souped up Fairlane that could lay a patch of rubber, even on the dry streets. I think that was after the famous "Macadam Road Accident"

Lon, Mike Hanlon, and Doug Orn were skipping school on one fine spring afternoon. They might have had a few beers to enhance their driving skills, I don't know. I wasn't along on this drive.

But long, windy, Macadam Road was pretty unforgiving if you were too heavy on the pedal. It was fun though, to take it close to the threshold of speed. Everybody was looking for a thrill.

It was like one of those "TV" type car crashes, that we used to replicate with my bicycle when Lon's Mom's Fury left Macadam Road for the steep, wooded dropoff of this "Deadman's Curve".

The Plymouth rolled once, twice, three times or more before it halted with a thud, probably 30 feet down from the street.

Stunned, as they gazed at the brush and knocked down saplings through radiator steam, they did a body count.

"You all right?" Lon asked.

"Yeah, you okay?" Mike questioned

"Yeah, you okay?" Doug repeated.

It could easily have been their last ride, but thankfully they were all okay. Mrs. Shankel's Fury, not so much. I'm sure that Lon got a little bit of his Mom's "Fury" when he told her what had happened to him and her car.

But it was a great time for cars. When we talked about "classic cars", we were probably talking about Model "A" s and Model "T" s.

What they refer to today as classic cars? At that time, we were driving them.

I think it was far cooler in those days to have a GTO than a 57 Chevy. If you had a 50s car, it was said you were driving around in an "Old Beater". 65 Mustangs and Road Runners didn't turn heads driving down the road. They were common.

You didn't need a computer or have to be a brain surgeon to fix your car in the 60s and 70s. We'd learn the basics of carburetion, ignition and exhaust in Auto Shop class. And from there, if you couldn't fix your car, your buddy probably could. And if he couldn't then your Dad was likely able to figure it out.

Sanding your points with the sandpaper off of a matchbook or blowing out your fuel filter would frequently put a dead car back on the road. Finding your most ignorant friend and asking him to hold a spark plug wire as you cranked the engine would not only let you know you had spark, but it would wake up your friend, and style his hair at the same time.

Trying to keep our old clunkers on the road, we spent a good amount of time at the Parts Stores. The closest store was Big Wheel Auto Parts, up on Highway 99.

I dreaded going there.

The parts counter guy was a mean looking, grubby guy who seemed to like no one.

He never smiled or said "hello" to anyone. He was overweight, with heavy stubble on his face. He never stood, but he had sat behind the counter on a stool for literally years. Without ever moving, I think. When you approached, he'd glare at you and growl,

"What make?"

That was the first of a dozen questions.

"Engine size?"

"Standard or Automatic?"

"Power Steering?"

"Air conditioning?"

"Two or Four door?"

"Hardtop or Convertible?"

"Color?"

"Solid or two tone?"

"Tape Deck?"

The questions went on and on....

Finally down to business, he'd ask, "Okay, what do you need?"

"An Air Freshener...."

"Playboy or Tree...?"

"Pine or New Car?"

I don't know why Shucks could get you just what you needed, with only half of the questions. And they said, "Hello" and "Thank you" too.

But they were further away, so most of the time we had to deal with "Mr. Big Wheel". No big deal.

No one thought much about fuel economy or air pollution. Gas was cheap and we all thought the air was supposed to smell like gasoline and exhaust. There were a few economical cars around like the VW Beetle, the Toyota Corolla and the Datsun (later to become Nissan).

But driving them was even more square than driving a 4 door Ford Galaxy around. Except for the VW Bug. There was a small faction who thought they were "cool".

Besides, we loved those big, boxy, gas guzzlers for the safety factor too. Japanese cars were considered dangerous amid the freeways packed with our heavy, thick walled cars.

Driving a Toyota was like sending a scrawny, skinny kid out in the ring with Sumo wrestlers. The prevalent view was that you wanted to be surrounded by a lot of metal in case of an accident.

Plus, Detroit was number one. It seemed unpatriotic to drive anything but an American car. Why there was nothing more American than burning rubber in your big gas drinking Chevy. In fact, their advertising pitch was "Baseball, Hot Dogs, Apple Pie and Chevrolet"

"Give 'em an inch and they'll take a mile" is an expression that we heard many times. Highway speed limits were 70 miles per hour. Which meant that you could get away with doing 80. But if you were in a hurry, that wasn't enough. So cars often went 85 or 90, until you saw a State Trooper by the side of the road.

As with "hot rodding", Dad had said "If you get a ticket, I'm taking your keys away". With a disclaimer. "I want you to go with the flow of traffic. If the traffic is moving at 80, and you get a ticket for doing the same. I'll let you off the hook. But I want you to be honest about it..."

I remember my first ticket in my 65 LTD.

"Did you know how fast you were going?" the Trooper asked

"No officer" I replied innocently.

I really didn't. The speedometer cable was broken. I was coming back from the ocean, and all I knew is I was making excellent time.

"You were doing 85 when I clocked you and slowing down at the time. "

I was just going with the flow of traffic. My car was doing 90 on the nearly evacuated stretch and I was just going along with the flow of what my vehicle was doing. But it didn't matter at the time. I was over 18 and not under Dad's thumb anymore. Not his problem anymore.

He'd done all he could to keep me driving responsibly. And I'm glad he did. But having tarnished my perfect driving record, I started a pattern of just before a ticket would go off my record, I'd get a second one.

This continued until I was about 25 years old and decided to follow the speed laws rather than pay more for insurance each time. But that wasn't until the 1980s. And that a whole 'nuther book.

25

WHAT MADE TUKWILA FAMOUS

As of today, Tukwila is slipping a little bit in its notoriety. Falling from the record books as "The most dangerous City in America", Tukwila has plummeted to number two.

Hopefully, the trend will continue, and it will once again be the peaceful, safe Land of the Hazelnuts where children could romp freely. Rather than the land of the Crazy Nuts who force them to stay inside. I wouldn't hold my breath for it though. Tukwila is a far cry from where we sat on the danger index in my day.

But there were several noteworthy developments in the 1960s that helped put Tukwila on the map.

When Southcenter mall floated up from the wetlands and swamps in the Tukwila lowlands, it was at the time, the world's biggest shopping center under one roof.

"It's always a beautiful day" was their advertising slogan. And all the kids would heartily agree.

It was fancy, air conditioned, and a great place to hang out and meet your friends from school. Southcenter was also home to Farrell's Ice Cream Parlor, DJ's Records, and Hickory Farms.

Like cattle, my friends and I would graze on the samples at Hickory Farms. Until they would fence us off and ask us to mosey on. Who said the best things in life weren't free?

I'm sure Southcenter is now but a midget in the biggest shopping center contest. But it was the friendliest of Giants in it's heyday.

I'm pretty sure that this next record still stands.

In 1969, a former Foster High School student and disgruntled ex-Marine, Raffaele Minichiello, commandeered a TWA flight from Fresno to Rome, in the world's longest hijacking.

After earning a Purple Heart fighting against the Viet Cong, Minichiello claimed the Marines had cheated him out of $200 in a savings account, and he was angry. I guess boarding a flight with a stick of dynamite, a M-1 Carbine, and a knife is one way to let off a little steam. I doubt he would have made it through the security checks these days.

Since Tukwila was kind of a satellite of Seattle, we'll take credit for some of its fame too.

The Ventures, Quincy Jones, and Jimi Hendrix, were all products of the "Jet City" as it was called before it became the "Emerald City".

Of course, Jet City was a reference to Boeing. And our planes have circled every inch of the atmosphere. We also sent our ashes around the world when Mt. Saint Helens exploded.

Boeing was a huge part of Seattle and Tukwila culture. When they prospered, so did everyone around here. In addition to being the leading manufacturer of airplanes, Boeing factories were also churning out satellites, missiles, and weapons for the cold war.

The Super Sonic Transport (the SST) was a big shot in the arm to the Seattle economy, until the program was canceled in 1971. We chuckled at the humor of a billboard that read, "Will the last person leaving Seattle turn out the lights?" While we shuddered at its truth. The cancellation washed away 70,000 jobs in the Puget Sound area.

Later, Seattle gave the world Heart, Nirvana, Soundgarden, and Starbucks Coffee.

Then, Boeing's management took the train to Chicago, leaving its orphans to build its planes in Renton and Everett. In doing so, Seattle lost that "we're all in this together" family relationship between Seattle, and its favorite airplane company.

Along with the loyalty that was lost when Daddy Boeing became a distant relative living in the Windy City, their "Our employees are our most valuable asset" slogan went out of style too.

We continue to make airplanes here, but without the same spirit and dedication that once flourished. The Boeing family would never be the same again.

But I say that Tukwila's biggest claim to fame, was it was the absolute best place in America for a kid to grow up in. And the quality of fun we had back then, still rivals any place today, or at any other time in history.

26

RITES...AND WRONGS

Growing up has always been a collection of firsts. You start with your first steps, your first birthday, first Christmas, first day of school, and your first bike. Then comes drinking your first beer, smoking your first cigarette, having your first kiss, and driving your first car.

There are many more of course, but each of these supposed landmarks of "progress", moved you closer (in your mind), to the goal post of being "grown up".

As you climbed up the ladder of these rites of passage, you also ascended in your social ratings among your peers. Later you would recognize the folly of some of these questionable firsts. But in our youth, the acceptance gained from checking these experiences off your list, was critical to your status.

Needless to say, there was a lot of lying involved in convincing everyone that you were "experienced", in the "love department"

By the time we were 15, every boy said they had not only kissed a girl, but would testify that they were regular Don Juan's, or Hugh Hefners, according to their own sworn statements. Perjury was prevalent.

Some claimed they'd "gone all the way" as early as age twelve.

But since everyone knew everyone in our little town, it was a hard fib to authenticate.

So, when pinned down about with whom or where you had gotten some "action" with, the guys had to think quickly.   And spin a tale about some imaginary rendezvous on vacation, in some faraway place, with a fantasy girl described in vivid fictional detail.

I actually got my first real kiss in the luck of a spin. A buddy up the street was having a party with a couple girls over and on the night's agenda was the game of "Spin the Bottle"

I'd heard of this game before.   But the only variation that I'd heard of, was where if the bottleneck chose you, you had to remove an item of clothing.   While I was hyped about the prospect of watching the girls disrobe, I didn't relish the thought of myself becoming a Chippendale.

As a fat kid, I was painfully bashful about my own appearance without clothes. Extremely self-conscious, I considered asking if I could just watch, but I didn't want to be labeled a "chicken" or a "square"

Before I had to peel down to my fruit of the looms, I was a little relieved to discover that their version of spin the bottle was just a kissing game,

Still, I wondered what would happen if the bottle chose two guys in a row? I was awfully glad to hear the clarification that in such a case, it would be a re spin until it matched a boy and a girl together.

Rites of passage aside, I would have had to bow out of the game, if it required kissing my buddies. Many people would say, "I'll try anything once". But not me. I never felt the urge to kiss another fellow.

As I won the spin, I was soon fully enjoying a long, passionate

French kiss with a pretty girl that I barely knew. The only awkward part was that, she was my buddy's girlfriend. You could only take it so far, without a foul being called.

Nevertheless, I made up for lost time. Making out was making me become aroused. But I suppressed my excitement, by imagining being at a ball game at Sick's Stadium. At least, I almost made it to second base.

Unfortunately for me, it would be a long time before I got to step up to the plate again.

Other tests of maturity, like smoking cigarettes, were dreaded by me. I hated the smell of cigarettes and my logic told me there was no upside, except the respect you would gain for the courage of trying the taboo. The risks were substantial, and the rewards few. Yet, to convince the others that you're not a "chicken" or a "square", you had to try it.

Smoking was even worse than I had imagined, Coughing and choking was not my idea of a good time.But somehow, the need for acceptance trumped my good sense. And through time I got snagged in the mousetrap of nicotine addiction. I persisted until I got hooked. In retrospect, the price of popularity is far too high if you must risk sacrificing your health in the bargain.

Not far away from Foster High School was a rundown shack they called the "Smoke-Hole" where kids would congregate to smoke between classes and at lunch time.

The thing I most remember about the smoke hole, was a rather clever graffiti slogan scrawled on the crumbling wall. It was prior to the Nixon / McGovern election, and it had a humorous political message.

"Don't change 'Dicks' in the middle of a screw, vote for Nixon in

72". While I favored McGovern, I did think the saying was rather witty.

Many of the girls would smoke right in the school bathrooms, occasionally getting caught. But you hardly ever smelled smoke in the boy's restrooms. No matter where the kids smoked, it was much "cooler" to be a smoker at that time, than it is to sport an oxygen tank from emphysema decades later. But we lived for the moments, not the future.

Alcohol was a no brainier to me. I always knew I would drink at some level. All the parents did, and it was widely acceptable to do so. If caught, there would be a certain amount of grace and understanding granted to your sin.

Drinking and eating are common to all humans. If the drink was somewhat intoxicating, oh well. Keggars either in someone's house when the parents were gone for the weekend, or out in the woods somewhere were big social occasions.

Most of us outgrew the novelty of getting snookered as a pastime. But some of us did find our fun became a battle as we fought off alcoholism. For them, just like smoking, what started as harmless fun evolved into an insidious slavery.

As much as I had eschewed the thought of becoming a cigarette smoker, from about mid-grade school I had always expected I would try marijuana someday. I had seen enough of the exaggerated anti-drug campaigns to realize they were not telling the whole truth and nothing but the truth.

Refer madness was not what I witnessed in observing those who had tried it. Unlike tobacco, there was a tangible benefit. The experience of getting stoned. But it was illegal and certainly parents didn't understand the allure of "grass" as we called it. I felt the "establishment" had deceived us by overstating the dangers of marijuana.

We didn't know how to get it, but we were bound and determined to find a way to get stoned. Around 7th grade I began hanging around with Delbert. His parents both worked, and the unfinished upstairs was his domain exclusively.

He was committed to his mission of getting his hands on some REAL pot. But in the meantime, he was raiding his Mom's flowerpots to find something smokable that would get him high.

Delbert dried and rolled the leaves of every potted plant in the house but found himself un-stoned in the haze of flower smoke wafting in the attic.

There were news reports of people smoking dried banana skins to get loaded too, so he peeled many of those looking for that elusive buzz too. I think he got a little extra potassium in his lungs, but he never got off.

He also tried smoking oregano, but it just made the upstairs smell like they had burned the pizza at the Italian restaurant. He claimed he got a little stoned by firing up a catnip joint, but I think he just imagined the high. But it did piss off his cat, as the kitty watched his stash go up in smoke.

Stoned or not, Delbert enjoyed a good practical joke. He loved phone pranks and invented a couple classic ones. Once he searched the white pages for someone named "Dunn". Calling them up in the wee hours of the morning he waited for the groggy answer on the other end of the line.

" Hello..." the rudely awakened man yawned.

"Are you Dunn?" Delbert asked.

"Yes"

"Well, then flush the toilet and go back to bed" Delbert shouted as he slammed down the phone.

Dunn's annoyance was a small price to pay for the laughter that we all got from that call.

Another time he decided to place an unwanted order for the Kirby's who lived next door. Delbert called 6 taxis and some chicken delight into their address. It was hilarious to watch the convoy of cabs pulling up to the confused Kirby's from the attic window.

Eventually, I think it was Lon who obtained some real grass. Probably from one of the bad boys who lived down by Central School. It was cheap Mexican marijuana, sold by the once "lid" (named for the baggies that had a flap to seal the bag) for only $5.

We did get stoned on that, and it was enjoyable. Kind of like drinking was. It made us kind of hungry though. We would each devour a whole frozen Banquet cream pie after polishing off the joint on a roach clip.

I burned out on pot early, as the paranoia that some experience was more like a psychosis to me. I'm kind of glad, because having not such a good time with marijuana, kept me from experimenting with the harder stuff.

If I couldn't handle marijuana, I surely didn't want to dabble with LSD or other hard drugs. With me, I might have never come back from my trip.

In my first real "band" with the Pastor's son Mark, he and I were jamming in the sanctuary of his Dad's church. We had both plugged into a Fender Twin reverb amplifier, when his older brother Jon and a friend burst in. They walked up to us and made a big show as they unfolded some wadded-up foil, revealing a half dozen, little white pills.

"What is that" I asked hesitantly.

"It's ACID man.... Here try one…" Jon smiled.

"No. I don't want any of that" I blurted, in shock.

"Come on man" he coaxed, popping one of the sinister looking tabs, and passing another to his friend.

"No. It's just not for me, man" I insisted

"Aww... You chicken..." He laughed as he handed one to his brother Mark, who downed it instantly.

Within minutes, they were all trippin' out. Seeing fantastic hallucinations, and babbling nonsense. I was scared, and stunned that these Pastor's kids were standing on the altar of their Dad's church, out of their minds on an unholy, LSD trip. Suddenly, Jon became alarmed an agitated.

"Oh man, I think I hear the cops coming" he said.

I was as sober as could be, and more frightened than I had ever been. Soon I thought, we'll all be in prison. Those three, for felony drug charges, and me as an accessory, in the cell with them. Then, all 3 of them burst out in hysterical laughter. What is so funny? I wondered. We're all doomed.

"You guys need to get rid of that stuff RIGHT NOW" I plead.

"Why? You can't get busted for Vitamin C" Jon cackled.

But passing those "Rites", wasn't just about kissing and substance abuse. Some of it was a little bit criminal. Pastor's son Mark, brought me along on a stealing trip to a construction site once, up in Renton where he lived.

Again, I was just along for the ride, but in my mind, I was guilty by association. Mark stole a barricade and a couple orange construction cones. He handed me a cone and I helped him hide the "loot" at his hideout in the woods. But I didn't want to be involved at all. I felt bad that I was a participant. Yet I also felt bad that I was such a square, who didn't want to be a part of stealing.

So later in Tukwila, I ran off with a construction cone of my own from a local road project. Terrified, I ran as quickly as a fat kid could off into the woods and hid it well beneath some brush. Believe it or not, over the next couple of days my conscience bothered me so bad, that I took my chances and snuck the cone back, leaving it where I got it.

So, I had passed the "larceny rite" although I had recanted. I just wasn't brought up to find any justification for stealing.

Similarly, I was once hanging out with some hoodlum acquaintances from around Central School, and we were all hiding on a bunker behind heavy shrubbery. The older guys were shooting out streetlights with a BB gun, and throwing rocks at cars.

I felt uneasy being there, and didn't want to be either a vandal nor an accomplice. I couldn't leave immediately because they would have thought I was going to rat on them. But at my earliest chance, I made some excuse and bailed.

While I failed this "vandalism rite", I didn't feel bad. I felt better that I had kept my integrity badge intact. Searching the far limits of my brain, I could find no provocation for a thrill at destroying things that didn't belong to me.

Sometimes rites are just plain wrong. And no matter how uncool it was, it felt right to lose those rites.

27

HIGHER EDUCATION

It was hitting the big time as my class left Tukwila Elementary and returned to Showalter which was now a Jr High School in 1967. The familiar faces of friends we'd spent our entire childhood with, were lost in the crowds as we blended in with the kids from grade schools throughout the district.

No longer, would we be shepherded through the curriculum by a single teacher for the year, but we had 6 classes to attend. locker combinations to remember, and of course. Bremmer's Hill to climb once again.

We were the "punks" as 7th graders, and during the confusion of this new world with more responsibilities, we were hazed by our upperclassmen. It was easy to feel lost, not only finding your classes, but finding your position in the pack.

The little girls from grade school had abandoned their pigtails and Bluebird uniforms, for makeup and jewelry, and were beginning to look like young women instead.

And the boys had started to grow hair on their pits. I was a late bloomer, kind of a child among adolescents and the culture shock made me feel a bit out of my zone. My pits were hairless.

Mr. Ridder and Mr. Weber were still there.   But a little less intimidating than they were when we were in Kindergarten and the First Grade. Still, they did their best to keep everyone in line. "Comb that hair", "Tuck in those shirttails", they still commanded.

In the real world, feminists were burning their bras. The young ladies at school, were crusading for the right to wear jeans.

It's hard to imagine today, but the problems in our halls were not of violence, or shootings. But instead, whether girls should have the right to choose between skirts or jeans. It was a hot pants issue at the time, and I think it took a landmark decision by the school board before the females found their emancipation, in a pair of Levis.

There was also a debacle about whether girls ought to be allowed to wear "fishnet" stockings to school. I was enthusiastically in favor of it. But the prudish powers that were, seemed to think they were too risqué. What a bunch of squares!

Academically, Junior High and High School were the good, the bad and the ugly. It was good to have a wood shop class. And our school bands were a lot better with the addition of the big horns and saxes as well as percussion tools.

History was good too, for sleeping. I really caught up on my sleep as the teacher lectured in his soothing monotone. Math was bad as they expected me to understand the abstract principles of Algebra.

But PE in Junior High was downright ugly. As I rediscovered why I'd given up sports in grade school.

I remember Mr. Tyler assigning the teams for Basketball.

"Sweeney...You're on the skins"

The last place on earth the school's "fat kid" wanted to be, was shirtless in the gym, just as the girl's PE class happened to be walking by the basketball court.

I heard the giggles from the girls across the gym as both the basketball and my chubby chest were bouncing along with the dribble. Those painful laughs from the amused young ladies, echoed like cackles from a flock of crows in my sensitive ears. How could I ever show my face at the dances?

Yet I did. Early dances were held after school with a record player spinning the hits of the day. The boys lined up on one wall of the small gym, and girls on the other one, looking each other over. There was much hesitation.

A lot of the guys were too bashful to ask a girl to dance. So initially there was more standing around bobbing our heads to the music than dancing.

Sometimes, the girls would ask a guy to dance, as many of the boys were just too shy. That never happened to me. And I assumed that if I ever got up the nerve to ask any girl to dance, she would just laugh at me and turn me down.

Eventually, I found my courage, and did ask a girl to take the floor with me. And to my astonishment, she said okay.

There was a widely used expression back then, calling one another a "Spaz", short for a spastic. I had no idea how to dance, but I just started weaving back and forth throwing my arms around waddling like a penguin. I think that I looked like a Spaz, but it really didn't matter. I realized it wasn't a relationship or a lifetime commitment, it was just a dance.

As pathetic as my position was among the fairer sex, there was one angel of light among the dismissa that l I felt from most of the girls at school. Lorraine Mikami actually used to flirt with me.

She would come up, put her arm around my shoulders and

whisper sweet words in my ears. "You're so cute" She HAD to be teasing, I thought.

In my insecurities, I wrote off her interest as being some kind of a big "put on". I figured that as soon as I would reciprocate, the whole school would bust out in collective laughter and a big "gotcha". Yet, she was persistent in her charms.

If I'd had a bigger brain, or more courage I would have taken a chance with her.Lorraine was pretty, and she had a great personality too. Plus, she demonstrated her sincerity in quite a few ways over the course of Jr High and High School.

She wrote the sweetest greeting in my 9th grade yearbook. I remember it verbatim.

"Oh Ed. Sweet, sweet Ed. There's not many guys left like you. Never stop being you. Sweet Ed- Love, Lorraine"

I guess I just couldn't take a hint

Then, when Lorraine got a job waitressing at a local restaurant, I stopped in one night. After finishing my dinner, she made me an extra big Sundae with extra everything, and triple cherries on top. On "the house".

I was so stupid! Yes, I was fat. Yes I had very little social skill. But this girl was even bribing me! It was a no brainier. And so was I.

What was my problem? I just couldn't believe any girl was really showing an interest in me.

"If you snooze, you lose", "You gotta play to win", "Nothing ventured, nothing gained" The list of appropriate sayings goes on and on. Naturally, Lorraine wasn't going to hold out forever waiting for me to respond to her affections. So, after a while I watched her walking hand in hand with a kid from my class.

Clearly, I blew it. I'd been handed the winning lotto ticket, and all I would have had to do was to cash it in. Damn that Punky Summers!

There were probably other girls who had shown some interest in me. But obviously, not as obviously as Lorraine had. My hopes of a romantic conquest were buried far too deeply in my own self-consciousness about being fat to let me see past my protruding belly at the opportunities before me.

But regardless of my lack of success with the chicks, I did manage to find the "highs" in Jr and Sr High School. While the football team was making tackles in the grass, we were smoking it, and drinking "Mad Dog" and "Bail Hai"

I think it was in the summer before we entered Jr High, when Lon Shankel showed me that Dandelions were for more than just mowing.

His Dad had turned their yard into a vineyard of sorts, by fermenting those hated yellow blooms into quart after quart of dandelion wine, in Mason Jars on his basement shelves. That's where I got the fuel for my first drunk.

It must have been a bumper crop that year because Lon's larceny of a half dozen jars didn't arouse any suspicion. I'd never had any alcohol besides an occasional sip of Dad's beer, but I always figured someday I would partake. I had no idea what to expect.

Hiding in the woods, Shank uncapped a jar and we chugged it down like desert nomads who had come across an oasis. My head swooned with dizziness, and everything seemed as funny as I felt.

Especially hilarious, was seeing the Goodyear Blimp puttering across the western horizon that night. I'd never seen any Zeppelins floating around in Tukwila before, so for all I knew, I was hallucinating.

"Are you SURE, this is just DANDELIONS?" I chuckled.

Until I had my frightening paranoia episode from a chunk of "Granddaddy Hash" (Or maybe it was "Blonde Lebanese") we used to toke on a little pot, to mellow out our stressful lives in academia.

Some of my friends also tried Peyote Mescaline, Magic Mushrooms, Uppers and Downers. But all that stuff frightened me. In Irish tradition, after my brief trial subscription to the Cannabis Club, I was strictly a lush.

With his glasses and sideburns, by age 16 Lon had become known as the "Professor". And professors never got "carded" when buying booze.

So, if anyone had the cash, we had no problem getting a rack of Schmidt "Animal Beer" or Rhinelander (which was thought to be Rainer Beer in a bargain label) Or a bottle of Annie Green Springs or Strawberry hill wine.

When it came to fine wines, Bali Hai was my drink of choice.

There were parties every weekend somewhere, and the beer was always flowing from the tap of a keg. For a couple dollars to get in, you could drink yourself into a pool of vomit that night, and have a nice hangover to greet you the next morning. What a deal!

I don't think I ever saw a high school football game through sober eyes. It was as natural as a hot dog at a baseball game, to kill a bottle of whatever we had before the kickoff. The radio declared that "things go better with Coca Cola" But they went even better with some 151 mixed in.

I avoided homework at all costs. Taking schoolwork too seriously. seemed counterproductive to my purpose in High School. Which was to have a good time.

If I'd been dumb, or if I had a heavy class load of college prep courses, I might have needed a study hall. But I was smart enough to pull "C"s and even an occasional "B", without trying. And I never seriously entertained the thought of college.

I was going to be a Rock 'n' Roll Star. So I took a study hall because it was an easy class to dodge and sneak off campus, skipping school.

Mostly, the study hall teacher, or adviser as they called them, could care less if we skipped. Once in a while they'd balk. But there was a legal way to get away from both study hall and regular school for a while. That was to explore colleges.

So, I'd tell them, "I'm going up to check out Highline Community College" or Green River. They'd smile proudly and pat me on my head and tell me to "Go" I actually did drive up and walk around both schools on a couple occasions. Highline seemed institutional and academic. But Green River looked downright cool.

It was surrounded by woods. They had a bunch of kids who looked like "Hippies" or "Stoners" smiling as they ripped open bags of chips and candy bars. "Ahh, the Munchies", I nodded, knowingly.

They had a far-out student run radio station, and the disc jockeys had that same,

"I just finished a doobie, and you just heard from Savoy Brown, and Grand Funk Railroad in that last set" drone like the guys on KOL Fm.

Who knows? I thought. If the rock 'n' roll thing doesn't work out, I might go for an associate degree. These seemed like people that I could "associate" with.

In both Jr High and High School, the athletics were revered. Before each game, we had pep rallies where the cheerleaders would lather the stands up to fevered frenzy. We went to state in Basketball one year and it was celebrated like the Super Bowl.

There were a lot of memorable teachers. Being a band nerd, one of my favorites was band teacher Mike McDaniel's (a third cousin of Jack McDaniels, I believe)

Mike was a Foster Alumni. He was somewhere in his 20s when he started teaching. And a very cool guy.

Like me, McDaniel's was kind of fat too. But he really had a passion for teaching music. He would have wanted to turn us into the Trans-Siberian Orchestra, except we weren't Russian, and we lacked both the dedication and the talent. There were a lot of apathetic, tone deaf musicians in the band.

McDaniels would sometimes get so mad, that he would break his baton on the music stand. With his veins popping out of his neck. He knew we could play this stuff well, if we would only practice.

He had a great deal of disdain for the caviler attitude of his percussion and drum section.

"Everybody thinks that drummers are cool, but they're the biggest squares in the world" I recall him saying.

Glad that I played the Baritone. Really, his heart was in the right place though. All he wanted was a little effort, so the kids would live up to their potential. It was a lot to ask of us.

As rebellious kids who were inching their way into the teens, many had big mouths that had grown even faster than their bodies had. They would test the limits, smarting off to the teachers. But at that time, teachers still had control of the classrooms.

I recall McDaniels slamming one kid up against the wall forcefully, when the kid got mouthy with him. The boy shriveled as

McDaniels taught him a serious lesson about respect. Shouting like a Drill Sargent up in his face.

He didn't sue or tell his parents. He just got himself in line. Some kids really just needed a good "Slamin'" occasionally.

Other teachers abused their power. An English Teacher who shall remain unnamed, was a rather mousy little man who had endured nearly constant harassment from his students.

His perched lips made him resemble a Perch or a Salmon. So, his students used to call him "Fish" and make fish faces at him as he tried to lecture.

As the tough kids and football players would sass him, he did his best to ignore their insults. But when the smallest kid in our class tried to join in on the fun, the teacher turned into Mighty Mouse, and grabbed him by the collar, for a ride up the middle of the blackboard.

When McDaniels did it, everyone including the kid that he threw, knew he had it coming. But when the "Fish" pounded the small boy against his wall, he lost what little respect he had from everyone in the class.

Besides Mike McDaniels, another of my favorites was Steve Escame. He was a small, young looking man who wouldn't look out of place mingling with the students in the hallway. But he was an easy going, devoted teacher and coach that made learning fun. I had him for my speech class and he was a great source of encouragement to me, and to everyone else in my class.

The shop teachers, Mr. Carpine and Mr. Merrifield were both just good old boys, the kind you might meet working in the Factory at Boeing in a few years. Rather than a rigid curriculum, they would be there to support whatever the interests of the students were with advice and coaching.

Every guy left school with a "foot" gas pedal and a "Playboy" plague he had cast in the metal shop foundry. And a nice wooden sign to hang on the house with his family name burned into grain. The racks in the auto shop were always full, with kids putting noisy headers on their cars.

The parking lot was like one of today's "car shows". Classic cars from the 50s weren't really that old back then, and there were quite a few cherry classics sitting out by the famous Foster rock each day.

Mustangs, Roadrunners, GTOs, and T birds were commonplace. Other than an occasional VE Beetle, all our cars had V8 engines with gas guzzling 4-barrel carburetors. Most had 8 track tape players blasting some rock'n'roll music.

Many would be seen on the weekend drag racing each other on the South Park Freeway. Or "moonin" pretty girls driving down I-5.

It was mandatory that each of these cars made a pilgrimage to cruise the Renton loop now and then. Kids came from everywhere to do the loop, and traffic was always thick on Friday and Saturday nights. Circling around, you would hope to bump into friends from school.

I never did too much academically or in sports. But as the Fat kid, I was nominated for the pie eating contest in one of our school competitions. Never one to race through my feedings however, I disappointed our class when I only placed 3rd.

But my girth also came in handy when I dressed up as Santa Claus one year.

Naturally we were all too old in High School to "believe" in Santa Claus, but for some unknown reason, I found myself "Ho Ho-Hoeing" it up in the halls.

Cheerleader Holly McGee was in her cheer uniform and took my hand and started running down the halls. Breathless, fat boy had a hard time doing my Santa laughs while being drug down the hallways by the fit, sprinting cheerleader, and I carelessly bumped into Chris Hansen. "Hey, watch where you're going, Sweeney" he growled.

Trying to stay in character, I responded with a hearty, "Ho, Ho, Hoe" and a big belly laugh. Somehow, I thought my costume gave me the power of invulnerability.

Chris wasn't amused, and I thought he was going to fight me right in the hallway. I soon learned that Santa wasn't Superman. If it had come to blows, what shame I might have brought to the Santa "brand"!

I don't mean to offend anyone, but I have to say that the Class of 74 was definitely, the coolest class at Foster, EVER. Probably ever since also.

We had the best jocks. Brad Sterling, Rusty Trudeau, George Howard, Gene Tashe. and a bunch of other guys whose names I don't remember took the Foster Bulldogs to the State Finals in basketball! That was the equivalent of the Mariners winning the world series! Top story on the world news!

Cheering them on were the prettiest Cheerleaders in the league. My memory may be a little fuzzy, but I seem to remember Kim O' Shaughessy, Charple Thomas and maybe Marion Woyvoditch shouting "We got spirit, Yes we DO...We got spirit, how 'bout YOU!"

Yes we did.

I hope I got the names straight, please don't sue me if you weren't a cheerleader. But when those girls shook their pom poms at them, the team exploded.

74' had some world class brains too. The Harvey Lockes, the Tim Larsons, and the Pam Andersons were bound for greatness. If world peace is ever achieved or cancer is ever cured, I'm convinced this brilliant Foster grads will be at the forefront of these miracles.

And we had our characters. I'm in no position to call anyone names, but EVERYONE called Greg Johnson "Porky". And he seemed to embrace the name. It wasn't out of meanness, just an affectionate name that was known throughout the Land of the Hazelnuts.

BG Lemon was indeed the class clown. He mentored me in comedy when I sat next to him in band. His impressions were remarkably authentic, and hilarious.

If you closed your eyes, you could swear you were sitting right next to Walter Brennen. Like Robin Williams, he had a wacky assortment of character voices he would pull out of his hat at the most opportune times.

And he could "hambone" even better than those guys on "Hee Haw".

Paul Pearl, God bless his soul, contributed the classic, facing backwards, "What are you DOING back there" pose to our senior class picture. Paul left us a few years ago, but his personality and wit will be remembered all our lives.

But the best thing about the class of 74' is our enduring relationships with each other. Even after 40 years, when we reunite, it's not just seeing old classmates. It's getting together with friends.

Maybe, I'm biased. No, NOT maybe... I AM biased. But I'll bet that every class from that era feels the same way about theirs as I do about my graduating class.

It was just something about growing up in Tukwila at that time.

Maybe it was something in the water. Maybe it was the something in the Hazelnuts.

As we neared graduation, it was rather bittersweet for all of us who had grown up together. Naturally we were anxious to get out into the world, but there was some melancholy at leaving behind the world we had known for so long.

Being a rather small school with between 100 and 150 students in our classes, everybody knew everyone at least a little. Some you would know quite well. Many of us spent all 13 years together sharing in thousands of experiences together.

But the future looked bright beyond school. Even for those of us who weren't college bound, opportunities were abundant.

The Alaskan pipeline was under construction, the shipyards and railroads were hiring. Boeing and Paccar were always looking for new people. Unions were strong and each of these avenues offered decent pay and great benefits. Comparatively, today's outlook for high school graduates appear bleak to me.

The military was actively recruiting offering great incentives and with the Vietnam war ending, it was likely you could learn a trade without getting shot. And get many perks that went along with Veteran status when you discharged. Many chose that route.

But as we threw our graduation caps and headed off to one last hellacious keggar at the Masonic Hall, it was the end of a long chapter of our lives and the beginning of new eras for each of us individually. And collectively, as a generation, a town and as a culture, the curtain closed on an unforgettable time of our lives.

EPILOGUE

I think all of us who were young in the 60s feel a kind of a kinship with one another and a connection to one of the most fascinating decades of all time. Unlike no other generation up until then, we were eyewitnesses to changes in the technology and the culture that laid the foundation of the future.

The sixties and seventies seem to me to have been a turning point in the history of the world. A cusp between the traditional society of the past and the futuristic world that we now dwell in. The triumph of those times was epic, and the tragedies were catastrophic, but the thrills of those days were unparalleled in my estimation.

To truly understand, you would have had to have been there. Each era has had its charms and its problems. To many of us, the troubles were few and the treasures were plentiful. We lived freely and safely, learned what we had to to become what we would be, and had the time of our lives while preparing for life ahead in a world brimming with opportunity. A world that no longer exists as we knew it.

It would be impossible to take our children or grandchildren on a tour of the Tukwila that we once knew. Along with payphones and real usable prizes in a box of Cracker Jacks, most of the places that we used to haunt have now vanished

Even the ancient artifacts of Rome and the Pyramids of Egypt serve as reminders of the lives people lived thousands of years ago. But with so many of our treasured landmarks now gone, there is

195

nothing left of them to preserve our legacy.

It's as though they destroyed the evidence that the cherished fabled adventures in our time had ever even existed.

Even the portal through which both myself and many others entered this world is now closed. Renton General Hospital was demolished and instead of babies, they delivered blue light specials of baby clothes as it morphed into a K-Mart. And with the passing of another generation it changed again into McLendon's Hardware. Kid's used to come fully assembled here. Now all you can get is parts.

Gone too are the full-service gas stations like Mac's Chevron where you could have your air and tires checked, and windshield washed while he filled your tank for only 25 cents a gallon. As you waited comfortably in your warm car. If you chose to get out, you could relieve yourself in a spotlessly clean restroom and buy an impossibly cold pop from the machine or get a road map for free.

These would also fix flats and do minor repairs. But for the heavy-duty car services you'd drive the extra mile to Knapp's Garage in Riverton.

It was like going to Gomer and Goober's shop in Mayberry. A true old fashioned garage that had probably seen more Model "A"s than Impalas. Knapp's had a rich knowledge of any mechanical problem you might face. But they too, are no more.

Kitty corner from Knapp's was Lee's Market. Not a full grocery store in the Safeway sense of the word, they had any essentials you might need for a breakfast lunch and dinner. With a Mom and Pop sensibility. Goodbye Mom and Pop.

Just up the hill on Highway 99 there was Salle's Market renowned for having a "live" Butcher. If there was nothing good on

TV like Leave it to Beaver" you could still watch the Cleavers in action up there. But not anymore.

Not far from Salle's you could dance up a storm at King's Diner toward Seattle or at White Shutters near Foster High School.

If you felt little bit country, you could circle back around to Interurban and have a regular hootenanny down at the "Riverside Inn" But the fiddles and guitars can't be heard there anymore.

Back up to the highway, you could stop by the tackle store and get yourself a can of night crawlers to fish Angle Lake with. Now you would have to dig your own.

Or swing by the Pancake Chef for a hardy Breakfast. Today, you'd have to go to IHOP instead.

Before Lunch, you might go shopping where "your dollar buys more", at the Wigwam store. Nowadays, you're out of luck. Go to Walmart in Renton.

Driving over to Renton, you couldn't pass up stopping at Gov Mart Bazaar. Even if you weren't buying anything, they had an automated doughnut making machine that would run the little dough rings through the boiling oil on a conveyor belt. You can't see that anywhere anymore.

But back to the highway. you might swing into the Lewis and Clark bowling alley and bowl a few frames before the movie starts right next door. After lunch at McDonalds of course, where burgers are only a Quarter.

After the show, if you were old enough, you could drop into My Place tavern for a beer, and more. For the guys, you could watch the topless dancers while you shared a pitcher of beer. And after 9, the topless girls left the stage for some live rock n roll bands and real women would come in and dance with you until closing.

It's still topless, but only because the sports bar that replaced it will never top the diverse entertainment that My Place offered.

If you were lucky enough to pick up a real girl at My Place, you could end the night with a late-night meal at 13 Coins which was open all night long.

Hey, what do you know? 13 Coins is still there.

So is McDonald's, but all you can get for a quarter is a packet of ketchup.

As the last Hazelnut tree falls in the land of the Hazelnuts to make way for yet another home improvement store, I can't say that my home town has really improved at all. I feel so blessed and lucky to have been placed on this planet when and where I was. It is today, the same place but a much different time.

You had to have been there.

DEDICATED TO

Terry Cox, Terry Mathison, Jim Webster, Mike Hanlon, Rocky Emmett, Ron Reeves, Ed Dowda, Mike Wing, George Howard, Albert Capps, Dennis Capps, Dino Ullakko, Lorraine Mikami, Paula Johnson, Paul Pearl, Doug Orn, and Kelly Cain and any other of our departed classmates that I might have missed.

Our Classes just aren't as classy without all of you....

Rest in Peace.

ABOUT THE AUTHOR

"Fast" Eddy Sweeney was born in the Seattle area in 1956. He grew up in Tukwila, and he thought the lifestyles of the 60s and 70s in that setting were worthy of a written account.

As a musician, a store clerk, and a Boeing crane operator, the Northwest has always been his stomping ground.

Although the area has changed dramatically since he and his friends used to roam the Land of the Hazelnuts, Tukwila and the surrounding areas will always have a special place in his heart.

Coming soon from Fast Eddy…

TAMING HERCULES

When Fred and Sharron Swanson freed a spunky, high spirited Alaskan Malamute puppy, from the prison of the local Animal shelter, they thought he'd make a good FAMILY dog. But that dog, had other plans.

Hercules thought that the Swansons would make him a good DOG family. With him, as the King of the Castle. Tenacious, even arrogant, Hercules was bound and determined to bark, chew, and dig his way to the top.

But after taking control of the Swanson's den, in his big shot dreams, Hercules aspired to rule the world.

In his first fictional book, Fast Eddy takes you inside the mind of Hercules. As he dreams of being leader of the pack, in his sleep. And into his life of Mischief and challenging authority during his waking hours.

It's a howl, and a tail wagging good time following the never-ending battle between man and dog. As the Swanson's attempt, "Taming Hercules"

Coming in June 2018

Made in the USA
San Bernardino, CA
24 December 2018